YORK NOTES

THOMAS HARDY

SELECTED POEMS

NOTES BY ALAN POUND

 Longman

 York Press

The right of Alan Pound to be identified as Author
of this Work has been asserted by him in accordance
with the Copyright, Designs and Patents Act 1988

YORK PRESS
322 Old Brompton Road, London SW5 9JH

PEARSON EDUCATION LIMITED
Edinburgh Gate, Harlow,
Essex CM20 2JE, United Kingdom
Associated companies, branches and representatives throughout the world

Quotations from Thomas Hardy's poetry are from *Thomas Hardy: Selected
Poems*, edited by Norman Page, 1998, published by Phoenix, a division of
the Orion Publishing Group

First published 2008

ISBN 978–1–4058–9622–1

Phototypeset by Chat Noir Design, France
Printed in China

CONTENTS

PART THREE
CRITICAL APPROACHES

PART FOUR
CRITICAL PERSPECTIVES

PART FIVE
BACKGROUND

PART ONE

INTRODUCTION

STUDYING POEMS

Reading poems and exploring them critically can be approached in a number of ways, but when reading a poem for the first time it is a good idea to consider some, or all, of the following:

- **Format and style**: how do poems differ from other genres of text? Does the poem capture a single moment in time, tell a whole story, or make a specific point?

- **The poet's perspective**: consider what the poet has to say, how he or she presents a particular view of people, the world, society, ideas, issues, etc. Are, or were, these views controversial?

- **Verse and metre**: how are **stanzas** or patterns of lines used to reveal the **narrative**? What **rhythms** and **rhymes** does the poet use to convey an atmosphere or achieve an effect?

- **Choice of language**: does the poet choose to write formally or informally? Does he or she use different registers for different voices in the poem, vary the sound and style, employ literary techniques such as **imagery**, **alliteration** and **metaphor**?

- **Links and connections**: what other texts does this poem remind you of? Can you see connections between its narrative, main characters and ideas and those of other texts you have studied? Is the poem part of a literary movement or tradition?

- **Your perspective and that of others**: what are your feelings about the poem? Can you relate to its emotions, themes and ideas? What do others say about the poem – for example, critics or other poets and writers?

These York Notes offer an introduction to Thomas Hardy's poetry and cannot substitute for close reading of the text and the study of secondary sources.

 CHECK THE BOOK

The Poetry Handbook by John Lennard (2nd edn, Oxford University Press, 2006) is a lively and accessible guide to the poet's craft and an introduction to practical criticism. It includes an excellent glossary of technical and scholarly terms and uses many examples from poems by writers Hardy admired, his contemporaries and those who were influenced by him.

READING THOMAS HARDY'S POETRY

Why, in 1895, did the 55-year-old Thomas Hardy turn his back on novel-writing and the London literary world, become a virtual recluse in his Dorchester home, and begin a second career as a poet?

Whatever the reasons which brought about these dramatic changes in his lifestyle and literary habits, Hardy certainly proved to be a prolific writer of poetry. Between 1898 and his death in 1928 he published over 900 poems, these being by his own account only a fraction of what he actually wrote. It is remarkable too that they included some of the greatest love poems in the English language: the series of **elegies** that Hardy, then aged 72, wrote for his wife Emma after she died in 1912. Why, though, did this outpouring of love and grief also convey such deep feelings of guilt?

Hardy is best known as the writer of **tragic** novels such as *The Mayor of Casterbridge* (1886) and *Tess of the d'Urbervilles* (1891). But as soon as we start reading his poems we are obliged to re-examine many of our assumptions about him: their content and form, as well as the circumstances of their composition, reveal **paradoxes** and inconsistencies which these Notes will address in more detail in subsequent sections. For instance, much of the continuing appeal of Hardy's poems, in an age even more sceptical than his own, is their universality. They deal with the things that are common to us all – birth, childhood, love, marriage, age and death – in honest, unsentimental, sometimes **ironic**, always thoughtful, and often moving ways. But they strike a chord in many readers precisely because of their lack of specificity and the absence of personal detail. Why, one wonders, is Hardy so reluctant to let us get close to him?

In fact, the poems are often less simple than they might at first appear, and Hardy himself remains an elusive presence in them. Indeed, much of the satisfaction to be gained from reading the poems comes from tracking the thought processes of the complex mind which lies behind them. Thus Hardy has a keen eye for the everyday experience of ordinary men and women in his poetry, but he is also profoundly aware of the mysteries of time and space, the forces of the universe which encompass human lives. Clearly, pessimism and **alienation** haunt Hardy's mind and poetry, but he offers – even as an old man – a determined resistance to them. The most memorable poems are those where Hardy seeks to restore human meaning and value to history and the landscape. How can we identify and, more crucially, how should we evaluate such material?

Hardy has often been seen as an **anachronism**, a **Victorian** who drifted into the twentieth century. This is misleading, even though the facts of his life story (see also **Background: Thomas Hardy's life**) might suggest otherwise: born in a remote hamlet before the railway had pushed into Dorset; achieving a level of success as a novelist which gave him entry into the highest levels of Victorian society; and, finally, dying in the same year that Walt Disney released the first Mickey Mouse films. But the truth is that Hardy's attitudes were shaped during the 1860s and 1870s and these were the years when the modern sensibility was being shaped, when the cherished beliefs of Victorian culture – about religion, history, politics, gender and so on – were crumbling, when Victorians began to see themselves as the victims rather than the masters of time, and as insignificant components in a vast and indifferent cosmic machine (see also **Critical approaches: Themes** and **Background: Historical background**).

Hardy is a complex figure because of his personal experiences and because he lived through turbulent times. Therefore we shouldn't, perhaps, be surprised to find contradictions and inconsistencies in his attitudes and outlook – but it is for these very reasons that he is such a fascinating subject. The assumptions of his rural upbringing were overlaid with the **ideologies** of Victorian middle-class culture, and both came into conflict with the radical ideas and attitudes he began to embrace as a young man. The tensions, even contradictions, which this gave rise to are evident in both his personal and his public life, and in his poetry. For example, he lost his faith but remained, according to his own account, 'churchy' all his life. He was an outspoken critic of Victorian middle-class society but he was eager to succeed in it. Although deeply pessimistic about

CONTEXT

Soon after Hardy's death, Macmillan published a 'biography' of Hardy in two volumes – *The Early Life of Thomas Hardy, 1840–1891* (1928) and *The Later Years of Thomas Hardy, 1892–1928* (1930) – purporting to be by his second wife, Florence Emily. In fact these volumes comprised Hardy's *autobiography*, and they are referred to as such throughout these Notes. Details of modern editions can be found in Further reading.

 CHECK THE BOOK

Robin Gilmour's *The Victorian Period: The Intellectual and Cultural Context of English Literature 1830–90* (Longman Literature in English Series, 1994) provides an introduction to the far-reaching changes in all areas of Victorian life during Hardy's formative years.

CHECK THE NET

The Thomas Hardy Association, **www.yale.edu/ hardysoc**, aims to 'promote the study and appreciation of Hardy's work in every corner of the world'. Of particular value are the links to 'notable [Hardy] websites' and the online forum 'Poem of the Month' where many of the poems mentioned in these Notes are discussed.

CONTEXT

Imagism was a self-conscious literary movement in Britain and the United States initiated by Ezra Pound and others around 1912. Imagists favoured short **lyric** poems couched in direct, concise language which were usually constructed around single images and focused on particular moments of experience.

the possibility of individual happiness, he continued to hope until late in life that the human race could make the world a better place (a hope which was destroyed by the First World War).

The mental turmoil of Hardy's formative years had a direct impact on the poetry he was to write some twenty years later. Indeed, it may be unlike almost anything else you have read. It mixes the simple and the sophisticated, the radical and the conventional, the familiar and the educated. It evinces feelings of loneliness and **alienation**, but strives to assert human meaning and value; it expresses dismay at the randomness of experience, while constantly searching for patterns; and, often written from the perspective of an old man, it plunders the past in order to revitalise the present. It employs specialised **verse forms**, as well as the more traditional ones found in **ballads** and hymns; and it mixes rural **dialect** with highly literary **diction**, often in the same poem. The sheer variety of Hardy's poetry, its spontaneity, and its wilful eccentricities – for Hardy thought polished writing was lifeless – are continually engaging.

Partly because of these qualities in his work, Hardy has been described as the first essentially twentieth-century poet. However, one of the most attractive aspects of his poetry is that it is so difficult to classify. It is clear that he is unlike his **Victorian** predecessors in many ways. He rejected what he saw as their 'smoothness'. Yet he doesn't seem to have much in common with the **modernists** such as T. S. Eliot and Ezra Pound, who were at the height of their powers before his death (see **Critical perspectives** and **Background**). We are not challenged by Hardy's poetry as we are by theirs to infer meaning from fragmentary forms, broken **images** and complex **allusions**. A much more illuminating way of seeing Hardy, and one which is examined in the discussions that follow, is as a major representative of a native English poetic tradition which has its roots in the ballad form and the oral tradition. This, for many readers, is precisely where Hardy's appeal as a poet lies.

PART TWO

THE TEXT

NOTE ON THE TEXT

Thomas Hardy's *Collected Poems* was published after his death, in 1928, and contained over 900 poems (of which about sixty had been written before 1890). The majority of these had been published in eight separate volumes between 1898 and 1928.

The edition of Hardy's poems used in the preparation of these Notes is *Thomas Hardy: Selected Poems* edited by Norman Page in the Everyman's Poetry series first published in 1998. The selection is arranged according to the order in which the poems were first published in the successive volumes. Two further poems, 'At an Inn' and 'The Haunter', which do not appear in this edition are also discussed. Both these poems are of course in *Thomas Hardy: The Complete Poems*, edited by James Gibson (Palgrave Macmillan, 2001) and can also be readily accessed online.

DETAILED SUMMARIES

NEUTRAL TONES

- Hardy recalls an early romance that came to an end by the side of a pond in winter.
- It was a first lesson in the disappointments of love.

The poet recalls the specific moment when, on a bleak winter's day, he and his love seemed to realise that their relationship was over. He says that the particular scene has come to mind – almost as a personal **motif** of the hazards of love – when later relationships have run into difficulties.

CHECK THE BOOK

Many of the poems discussed in these Notes appear in *Thomas Hardy: Selected Poems* (1993) edited by Tim Armstrong in the Longman Annotated Texts series. This is an excellent scholarly edition which has detailed notes on each poem (including a very useful description of its **metrical** scheme) together with a challenging critical introduction. Armstrong also includes an appendix of excerpts from Hardy's autobiography.

GLOSSARY

8 **On which lost the more** on the question of which of us lost more

CHECK THE POEM

Hardy considered the mind to be 'etched' (or engraved) by the memories of life events. There is a similar metaphor in 'In a Former Resort After Many Years'. Hardy also believed that an individual's experience was inscribed on the face (see 'Your Last Drive'), and that special human events could be inscribed on the landscape (see for example 'At Castle Boterel').

COMMENTARY

The controlling **metaphor** of the poem, first announced in the title itself, is of a picture – or possibly an etching – in 'neutral tones'. The scene is drained of colour; the sun is described as 'white' (2) and the few fallen leaves from the ash tree are 'gray' (4). This reinforces the key notion that the failure of the love relationship has drained the world of meaning: love dies (the woman's bored 'eyes', her false 'smile' and the inconclusive 'words' the lovers exchange – 5, 9, 7 – confirm how things have changed) and this corresponds to the death of nature. To complete the idea, at the end of the third **stanza** a **simile** likens the 'grin of bitterness' which crosses the woman's face to an 'ominous bird' (11, 12). The total effect of these details is to clinch the controlling metaphor: this dreary scene is inscribed on the poet's memory, and surfaces whenever he is again subject to love's 'keen lessons' (13).

The title also describes the poem's tone. For although the subject matter might have provoked an outpouring of feeling, this is in fact an emotionally restrained poem. Hardy keeps his feelings in check and, on the surface at least, tries to be objective. This kind of detachment is characteristic of Hardy. It is partly a self-protective manoeuvre, but it also shifts the poem into a more reflective mode, towards a consideration of the effects of the passage of time on human relationships. But the poem, which is generally very precise in its use of language, also contains some awkwardness of expression, notably in the third stanza. What, for instance, does 'thereby' (11) refer to? Such moments, it could be argued, betray the real confusion of feeling just beneath the poem's surface.

QUESTION

Look specifically at the **narrative** of 'At an Inn'. How is the story told and how does it compare with 'Under the Waterfall'?

AT AN INN

- A clandestine meeting between the poet and a woman ends in disillusionment.
- Many years later, however, and now separated, they long for the togetherness they lacked at the time.

A couple arrive at an inn, and are mistakenly thought to be lovers by the proprietors, who welcome the pair warmly. The truth is, however, that romance fails on this occasion. Years later, the poet looks back on that moment and reveals that he and his companion now long to be together – and in this sense *be* what they had only *appeared to be* on that earlier occasion.

COMMENTARY

While Emma Hardy was still alive Hardy formed a close relationship with Florence Henniker, a married woman, whom he had met in 1893. The relationship was carried on largely by correspondence, and Emma's awareness of it, and resulting jealousy, contributed to the growing estrangement from her husband (which Hardy describes in the *Poems of 1912–13*). This poem is based on a visit that he and Mrs Henniker made to Winchester together when they were taken to be lovers by the proprietors of an inn which in reality they were not. Having conventional Christian views, Mrs Henniker made it clear to Hardy from the start that the relationship could never be more than platonic although they remained close for many years. This may explain the tone of the poem as well as suggesting that the concluding stanza, where Hardy fervently wishes that geographical and legal barriers to his relationship with Mrs Henniker might dissolve, constitutes wishful thinking.

Ironies accumulate in this poem. The couple arrive as 'strangers' (1) at the inn in a double sense – both unknown to the proprietors and, it soon emerges, to each other. However, they are taken to be lovers and their hosts are both charmed by their presence and a little envious of their apparent 'bliss' (15). Things are not what they seem, however. In fact, as the **imagery** makes clear, there is something deathly about the relationship which 'chilled the breath / Of afternoon, / And palsied unto death / The pane-fly's tune' (21–4). It is significant, here and elsewhere, that the most imaginative uses of language in the poem describe the failure of love in contrast to the **clichéd** descriptions of the seeming-lovers. Love is **personified** as a malign influence in stanza 4, withholding his beneficence, giving the couple an aura of being lovers and then provoking real feelings of love only after they are separated. In this guise, Love can be identified with the web of fate, which, in

GLOSSARY

5 **opined** considered (i.e. were of the opinion that we were)

23 **palsied** stilled or (here) silenced (i.e. paralysed)

24 **pane-fly** the fly buzzing in the window

27 **hold** fortress

29 **port** bearing, manners (therefore, appearance)

 CHECK THE POEM

Other poems which deal with events in the relationship with Florence Henniker and its problems include 'A Broken Appointment', 'The Division' (where Hardy mentions 'that thwart thing betwixt us twain', 9) and 'A Thunderstorm in Town'. Mrs Henniker is probably the 'one rare fair woman' referred to in stanza 6 of 'Wessex Heights'.

CHECK THE BOOK

In his novel *Jude the Obscure* (1895) Hardy had attacked the marriage laws of the **Victorian** era as being, with the connivance of church and state, harmful to human happiness. Throughout the nineteenth century and into the twentieth stringent requirements for proving marital breakdown meant that divorce was very difficult to obtain for most. In a postscript to a 1912 edition of the novel Hardy states his belief that 'marriage should be dissolvable as soon as it becomes a cruelty to either of the parties'. The novel was bitterly attacked for its 'anti-marriage' doctrines.

GLOSSARY

11 **frame** body

11 **eve** the later years of the poet's life, the present, as opposed to the earlier prime of 'noontide'

Hardy's pessimistic view, governs (usually for the worse) individual lives and history.

The final **irony**, of course, lies in the assertion at the end of the poem that the couple, once mistaken as lovers, now really are so, although separated. The appeal to the 'laws of men' (39) to yield to the desires of the lovers makes sense of course in view of the fact that both Mrs Henniker and Hardy were married to other people. And the real feeling in the final stanza is denoted by the **anapaests** in lines 33, 37 and 40 in contrast to the rigid **metrical** scheme elsewhere in the poem which effectively locks up Love in spite of appearances to the contrary.

I LOOK INTO MY GLASS

- Looking into a mirror, Hardy reflects on the cruel irony that his ageing body still harbours the strong feelings of a much younger man.

The poet looks in a mirror ('glass', 1) and wishes that his feelings had decayed in the same way as his body. The distress he feels so acutely at the coldness of former friends and possibly lovers has denied him a peaceful old age. In the final **stanza** he blames the arbitrary processes of time which have wasted his physical being while his 'heart' (4) retains the intense feelings of his prime.

COMMENTARY

Hardy had lamented elsewhere the fact that human consciousness resides in the frail body. One consequence of his reading of Darwin (see **Critical approaches: Themes** and **Background: Historical background**) was the belief that consciousness was almost an accident in a material universe, and that this was the source of much human woe. This relatively slight **lyric** only hints at the bitter personal experience which informs it – the distress arising from the negative criticism attracted by *Tess of the d'Urbervilles* (1891) and *Jude the Obscure* (1895) (see **Background: Thomas Hardy's life**) and Hardy's estrangement from his wife. The causes of Hardy's gloom in the 1890s are revealed in later poems such as 'Wessex Heights'.

The opening **image** where the poet says he views his 'wasting skin' (2) in a mirror is characteristic of Hardy's work, suggesting the adoption of a somewhat detached, reflective attitude towards his own predicament. This impression is further reinforced by the suppression of personal details, which (as in 'Neutral Tones') is in part a self-protective manoeuvre but which also has the effect of universalising the poem's treatment of the effects of 'Time' (9). 'Time' is personified and thereby given a weighty and ominous presence in the poem – this contrasts with the **rhetorical** appeal in the first stanza to a God Hardy was unable to believe in.

The poem comprises four-line stanzas rhyming abab, in each of which lines 1, 2 and 4 are **iambic trimeters** and line 3 is an **iambic tetrameter**. This is a stanza form commonly used in hymns. Its deployment in such a sceptical poem has a clearly ironic effect.

DRUMMER HODGE

- The body of a young soldier is thrown into an unmarked grave in a foreign land.
- However, his corpse is magically transformed into a tree by the processes of nature.

Drummer Hodge, far from home and denied the normal funeral rites, is unceremoniously laid to rest in a crude grave. A native of rural Dorset and familiar with its landscape and night skies, he now lies forever in an alien terrain beneath 'Strange stars' (12). Moreover the poem hints, with considerable irony, that 'homely' (15) Hodge had only limited understanding of the political forces which led to his death in South Africa, and may actually have felt a closer affinity to the Boer farmers he had been sent to fight. However, Hodge's corpse becomes part of the natural processes of the South African

---

CONTEXT

In his diary for 18 October 1892 (and reproduced in his autobiography), Hardy wrote: 'I look in the glass. Am conscious of the humiliating sorriness of my earthly tabernacle ... Why should a man's mind have been thrown into such close, sad, sensational, inexplicable relation with such a precarious object as his own body!'

GLOSSARY

3 **kopje-crest** the summit of a small hill

4 **veldt** open grazing land

9 **Karoo** flat, barren land

10 **Bush** uncleared land

12 **gloam** twilight

In this poem, Hardy assumes a more public voice than usual. It was written in reaction to much more jingoistic poetry of the time, for example, 'The Transvaal' (1899) by A. C. Swinburne which includes the lines: 'Too long / Have sloth and doubt and treason bidden us be / What Cromwell's England was not ... / Strike, England, and strike home'.

CONTEXT

Hardy writes about the poignancy of war, in this case the Boer War of 1899–1902, a conflict between the Boers (descendants of Dutch immigrants) and the British for the control of South Africa. A note attached on first publication of this poem reads: 'One of the Drummers killed was a native of a village near Casterbridge.'

plain. In particular he is transformed into a tree – and in this way the dignity he was denied in death is reaffirmed.

COMMENTARY

The central **irony** of the poem – and the source of its poignancy – is that the simple country boy from Wessex is permanently transplanted to a foreign land. This is underlined both by the alien nature of the landscape in which he lies and, perhaps more significantly, by the unfamiliar (southern) constellations of stars which nightly appear in the sky over his grave. The use of Afrikaans terms in the first two stanzas – 'kopje-crest', 'veldt' and 'Karoo' (3, 4, 9) – enhances the poignancy of the situation: not only is the landscape strange, but the local terms for it would have meant nothing to Hodge.

We do not, in fact, know the drummer boy's real identity – 'Hodge' was a slang word for an agricultural labourer, and had all the demeaning connotations of 'country bumpkin'. Hardy hated such terms and was very critical of those who used them. The drummer boy's perfunctory burial hints at this kind of prejudice. In the light of this, perhaps we can say that the poem is not centrally about the waste and futility of war at all – after the brutality of the first couple of lines this theme is not developed (although there is an implied attack on British imperialism here). Indeed, the exotic vocabulary and the almost incantatory (song-like) references to the foreign stars and constellations at the end of each stanza (reminiscent of the refrain often found in **ballads**) have a quite different effect: Hodge, who will forever be 'portion of that unknown plain' (13), grows in stature, partly because his fundamental humanity is established in the face of the brute facts of the material universe ('strange-eyed constellations', 17) and partly because of the growing sense of wonder associated with his death ('His homely Northern breast and brain / Grow to some Southern tree', 15–16). In **elegising** Hodge by these means, and thereby affirming his individuality, Hardy challenges the **stereotype** of the yokel – and the discriminatory ways of thinking which lie behind it.

AT A LUNAR ECLIPSE

- Hardy is impressed by the spectacle of the lunar eclipse.
- It prompts him to reflect by contrast on the vanity of human activity on the earth.

Hardy is awed by the sight of the earth's shadow moving across the face of the moon. He wonders how to connect this tranquil **image** with the harsh realities of life on the planet. The pretensions of humanity are deflated by the eclipse – including the belief that the human race has an exalted role in God's plan. The authentic spectacle of the eclipse becomes a measure of the way the brutalities of war and intrigue are sometimes romanticised on earth.

COMMENTARY

In the first four lines of this sonnet Hardy communicates his sense of the majesty of the eclipse with the use of weighty **diction**: 'In even monochrome and curving line / Of imperturbable serenity' (3–4). He then wonders how to reconcile the serene shadow cast by the earth on the moon – 'That profile, placid as a brow divine' (7) – with what he knows of the strife and hardship of human society. In lines 9 to 11 he reflects on the **paradoxes** prompted by the scene: humanity is so self-important ('immense Mortality', 9) and yet the earth's shadow is so small; and it is also surprising that 'Heaven's high human scheme' (10) should apparently be circumscribed by the limited silhouette on the face of the moon. And here, of course, Hardy registers his scepticism about a Providential God with a plan for the growing good of the world. The poem concludes with the suggestion that the sublime eclipse offers an ironic judgement on human vanity. It is likely that the example of 'earthly show' (12) used at the end of the poem is a reference to the war between the Greeks and the Trojans: the beautiful Helen was carried off to Troy by Paris, son of King Priam, and the Greeks besieged the city for ten years in order to get her back. If this is the case, then the great events described at the end of the poem are seen ironically – motivated as they were by frivolous concerns.

 CHECK THE POEM

Hardy's enthusiasm for astronomy is also reflected in 'The Comet at Yell'ham' where again he relates the cosmic event described to human life. In the poem 'Afterwards', Hardy says he hopes to be remembered as someone who had an 'eye for [the] mysteries' (16) of the night sky.

CONTEXT

Hardy thought the glory of war was a thing of the past: 'The romance of war has withered for ever … Down to Waterloo war was romantic, was believed in' (letter to Arthur Quiller-Couch).

CHECK THE BOOK

The word 'stellar' (12) seems to have had particular resonance for Hardy as a measure of the cosmic loneliness of humanity. In the preface to his story of star-crossed lovers entitled *Two on a Tower* (1882) Hardy says that he has 'set the emotional history of two infinitesimal lives against the stupendous background of the stellar universe'. Similarly, in 'At a Lunar Eclipse', Hardy sees humankind and its vanities from the perspective of the immensity of space.

GLOSSARY

1 **coppice** area of dense undergrowth and small trees

5 **bine-stems** climbing stems of bindweed, perhaps jutting above a nearby hedge

10 **outleant** laid out (as a corpse prepared for burial)

'At a Lunar Eclipse' is a **Petrarchan sonnet**, a poem comprising an octet (first eight lines) rhyming abba abba and a sestet rhyming cde cde. It is a traditional form and chosen deliberately by Hardy. In part this is because the sonnet form offers a challenge to the poet to say all that he wants to say in fourteen lines. But probably more important for Hardy is the opportunity to offer a counterweight or antidote to the 'moil and misery' (8) and 'earthly show' (12) of human existence with a poem which is controlled, balanced and reflective – and, indeed, one which has something in common with the 'symmetry' (5) of the eclipse itself. It is common in a sonnet for there to be a transition from octave to sestet which coincides with a 'turn' in the argument or mood of the poem. Here the transition is not definite, in part because the questions prompted by the eclipse bridge octave and sestet. But it is evident that the profound emotions felt by the poet at the sublime spectacle of the eclipse at the beginning of the poem have been replaced by something bordering on contempt for the petty egotism of human affairs at its conclusion.

THE DARKLING THRUSH

- On a cold evening in winter, the dejected poet looks out across a barren, wooded landscape.
- The sudden hopeful song of an aged thrush, however, causes him to question his pessimistic mood.

The poem is set at the end of the day at the end of the year at the end of the nineteenth century (which, following much debate, had been officially dated as 31 December 1900). The overwhelming sense of things coming to an end in nature corresponds with the poet's dejected mood. The poet is alone in a frozen, desolate landscape; night is closing in; the century is passing; and the poet is 'fervourless' (16). Suddenly an 'aged thrush' (21) bursts defiantly into song, seeming to challenge all that has gone before. The surprised poet reflects on this. Does the thrush know something he doesn't? Is the poet's pessimism without foundation?

COMMENTARY

This is a poem which is richly suggestive in its choice of **diction** and deployment of **imagery**. The use of 'darkling' in the title, for instance, refers to both the thrush (which is literally in the dark) and the poet's state of mind as he reflects gloomily on the passing century. Hardy says 'The tangled bine-stems scored the sky / Like strings of broken lyres' (5–6), where the **simile** of the broken harps denotes the absence of joy and the collapse of faith. The funereal imagery in the second **stanza** is also striking. The description of the thrush in the third stanza is deliberately ambiguous: it is old and frail and in a sense emerges from the desolate landscape. Nevertheless, it sings joyfully.

Critics have often said that the message of the poem is indeed that the bird knows more than the poet, that its song confirms that the poet's pessimism is unfounded – that there is 'Hope' (31) which, if not presaging the return of God, at least anticipates the coming spring. However, a close reading of stanzas 3 and 4 makes this interpretation difficult to defend. The vigour of the thrush's song, though fully evoked, does not quite displace the melancholy picture which has gone before. Thus, while the thrush's 'full-hearted evensong / Of joy illimited' (19–20) bursts upon the scene, the bird is nevertheless 'aged … frail, gaunt, and small, / In blast-beruffled plume' (21–2); and in lines which perfectly embody the tension between positive and negative, the bird is said to 'fling his soul / Upon the growing gloom' (23–4). The tentative **syntax** in the final stanza ('That I could think there trembled through', 29) suggests that the poet remains unconvinced that there is any 'Hope'.

The overriding impression which the poem leaves is that the material world – here seen as an almost lifeless wasteland – remains utterly **alien** and threatening to the human consciousness (human beings merely haunt this place). In later poems Hardy is more successful in projecting human value and meaning onto the landscape (see, for example, 'At Castle Boterel'). But here we find a perspective much more akin to Charles Darwin's view of nature (see also **Critical approaches: Themes** and **Background: Historical background**): that it was a bleak place of struggle, without plan or purpose, but **paradoxically** also a site of astonishing creativity.

CHECK THE POEM

There is a long tradition in English poetry of poems about birds. These include poems by the early nineteenth-century **Romantic** writers Hardy admired: Wordsworth's 'To a Skylark' and 'To a Cuckoo', John Keats's 'Ode to a Nightingale' and Shelley's 'To a Sky-Lark'. Hardy's poem echoes these earlier poems – 'O blessed bird', says Wordsworth of the cuckoo, and 'Darkling I listen' (to the nightingale), says Keats.

CHECK THE POEM

There is an **allusion** here to Matthew Arnold's 'Dover Beach' (1867), a poem which deals with the intellectual malaise prompted by evolutionary thinking. Arnold compares the age to a 'darkling plain'.

THE RUINED MAID

- A chance meeting in town initiates a dialogue between Amelia ('Melia), the ruined maid, and an old friend of hers from the country.
- The friend is impressed by the way Amelia has changed since she laboured in the fields – but Amelia points out, somewhat ambivalently, that the improvements are the result of her having become a fallen woman.

CHECK THE BOOK

Many of the Manchester factory workers in Elizabeth Gaskell's *Mary Barton* (1848) are recent arrivals from the country. Pip, in Dickens's *Great Expectations* (1861) journeys from the Essex marshes into London – and wants to cast off his rural manners and **dialect**. The 1851 census showed that for the first time in history there were more people living in British cities than in the country.

Meeting her in town, Amelia's friend enthuses about her transformation into an urban lady: she wears fashionable clothes and adornments, she speaks in a more refined way, she appears to be healthier and she has a cheerful disposition. For her part, Amelia points out in the last line of each **stanza** that she is nevertheless 'ruined' – but her tone suggests that she is far from ashamed of it. She has lost her chastity and suffered the inevitable moral censure – but she feels that she is better off than when she was labouring in the fields.

COMMENTARY

This poem reminds us that Hardy can be comic – and make a serious point: here he both inverts the **pastoral** mode and deconstructs the idea of the fallen woman. Country life is no idyll for women, as the friend's words make clear; the town, by contrast, seems to offer many benefits to a girl who has been disgraced sexually.

The poem comprises six **quatrains** organised in parallel fashion: the first three lines convey the friend's compliments and envy, and the last Amelia's sarcastic responses. In this way, Hardy satirises the standard middle-class **Victorian** view of the fallen woman or prostitute as a social outcast – and raises more general questions about the status of women in his society. Ironically, Amelia seems to have achieved a voice of her own, a sense of personal integrity (regardless of the opinions of others), financial independence and happiness – conditions denied even to many middle-class women of the time. Paradoxically, of course, the only way Amelia has reached this privileged position is by selling her body – as her friend well knows. And though the friend is envious she is also critical. In part she wants what Amelia has; in part it frightens her. There is an implicit judgement when she says she is 'bewitched' (14) by Amelia's delicate cheek (is there a more sinister side to Amelia?), and desires to 'strut about Town' (22) (with a devil-may-care arrogance?) like her friend.

The poem disguises, or mutes, the truth about Amelia's position in Victorian society: she will never be able to go back, to her village, to her friends, to respectability. This is a scenario which of course fascinated Hardy and there are many characters in his novels who are in some ways 'fallen' – Michael Henchard (*The Mayor of Casterbridge*, 1886), Tess Durbeyfield (*Tess of the d'Urbervilles*, 1891) and Jude Fawley (*Jude the Obscure*, 1895) are outstanding examples from the later fiction. These characters can never 'go back' – or at least can never throw off their shame, or escape their past. They are caught in the web of fate, the predetermined plot of their lives, which they cannot influence. In this poem such fatalism is subordinated to the comic tone – a tone in large measure established by the **ballad** form, including the **refrain**-like last line of each stanza, and strongly **stressed** and decidedly upbeat **rhythm**. The tone of the poem also sustains Hardy's ambivalence about the fate of the maid, neither condemning nor condoning. Nevertheless, the dismal options for working women are glanced at here: hard labour or superficial independence as a rich man's mistress – or, of course, prostitution, in which case her freedom would be entirely illusory. In keeping with its comic tone, the poem is appropriately elusive about Amelia's actual situation.

CHECK THE BOOK

In *Tess of the d'Urbervilles* (1891), Hardy offers a different perspective on the fallen woman. As here, he does this by seeing things through the eyes of the woman herself. But this poem is much lighter in approach than the **tragic** novel. Hardy is explicit about the rigours of agricultural labour for women in Chapter 43 of the novel which shows Tess at Flintcomb Ash.

CHECK THE POEM

The hardships of Flintcomb Ash are also alluded to in the poem 'We Field Women', which has specific parallels with Tess's story.

THE SELF-UNSEEING

- This poem recalls a happy moment from Hardy's childhood when he danced to his father's fiddle-playing by the fire as his mother looked on.
- He now regrets that they all took the happy moment for granted at the time.

CONTEXT

In his autobiography, Hardy records that as a young man he was 'extraordinarily sensitive to music' and often danced to the music of his father's fiddle, sometimes being moved to tears by particular tunes.

CHECK THE POEM

Hardy writes on a number of occasions about not fully taking in the meaning of an event at the time, because 'we were looking away!' This regret is implicit throughout 'Lines: To a Movement in Mozart's E-Flat Symphony'. But contrast 'The Shadow on the Stone' where he *refuses* to look (behind) to see if Emma's ghost is actually there.

Hardy remembers the cottage where he was brought up. While his mother sat beside the fire, the young boy danced to the music of his father's fiddle. It is a memory tinged with sadness: not only is his father now dead (he in fact died two or three years before Hardy wrote the poem), but on reflection Hardy realises that neither he, nor his parents, appreciated the fullness of the moment.

COMMENTARY

This is a beautiful little poem. The memory of the family scene is only sketched in, but the details are telling. Indeed, the effectiveness of the poem depends on its economy of manner: not only does the moment come alive but its poignancy in retrospect is given a universal resonance. The flagstones (of which the floor would have been composed) are described as 'Footworn and hollowed and thin' (2), but the adjectives transfer to the human figures in the poem: the stones are almost as 'dead' (4) as those who once walked on them. This is to be contrasted with the last **stanza** which is – until the chastening reflection of the final line – irradiated by the firelight from stanza 2, as the memory and its meaning come into focus.

Alliteration (on the letters 'd', 'b' and 'g') plays a vital part in bringing this moment from the past alive. For one thing, it echoes the **rhythms** of the father's music and the child's self-absorbed dance. More specifically, in line 10 it draws attention to the word 'emblazoned' (10), at first glance an odd choice (with its heraldic associations) in this context, but on reflection wonderfully apposite: picking up the blaze from the fire in stanza 2, its suggestions of vivid and lasting colour give a particular resonance to the familial 'Blessings' (10) of the moment described. The idea is completed with the suggestion that 'Everything glowed with a gleam' (11) – not only literally, because of the light from the fire, but also figuratively, as in a painting which captures the extraordinary in an everyday domestic scene.

Hardy wrote elsewhere about his failure to grasp fully the meaning of the present moment. He seems to have thought that this was a common problem and part of the psychological malaise of the times in which he lived. But here – although he sadly acknowledges the inevitable processes of time ('dream', 'that day' and 'gleam', 9, 10, 11) all suggest the transience of the moment) – there is a triumphant reclaiming of the past and its significance in memory. This reclamation of the past is not only defiant of time's transience but also a means of regaining the present.

A TRAMPWOMAN'S TRAGEDY

- A pregnant woman misleads her lover into believing that his friend is the father of her baby.
- The deceived lover kills the friend in a fit of jealousy.
- The lover is hanged, but his ghost – unable to rest until it knows the truth – haunts the trampwoman, whose baby is stillborn.

The **narrator** and her companions – Mother Lee, Johnny and her lover – tramp through the countryside on a hot summer's day. In order to incite her lover's jealousy, on reaching an inn the trampwoman flirts with Johnny. Angry, her lover asks whose child she bears, and on a whim ('to tease', 64) she lies and says it is Johnny's. On hearing this, her lover stabs Johnny to death. For this he is hanged. Now alone and friendless, the woman gives birth to a stillborn baby. In a dream the restless ghost of her lover comes to her and asks whether the child was his or Johnny's. She tells him that after they became sweethearts she did not sleep with any other men. Satisfied, her ghostly lover then slips away from her forever.

COMMENTARY

This poem demonstrates Hardy's confidence in emulating the **ballad** form. The trampwoman's voice, the economical narration, the refusal to examine motive or apportion blame – all establish a feeling of authenticity, as do the skilfully contrived stanzas, the effective **refrain** and the **rhyme scheme**. But this story is quite explicitly set in Wessex (see **Background: Hardy's Wessex**): the

GLOSSARY

7 **fosseway** sunken road

7 **turnpike** toll road

15 **landskip** landscape

31 **tap** inn

45 **tor and lea** hill and meadow

49 **settle** wooden bench with a high back

80 **Ere his last fling he flung** before he was hanged

CONTEXT

In his autobiography Hardy says this is 'a ballad based on some local story of an event . . . which took place between 1820 and 1830'. Blue Jimmy was a horse thief active in Wessex in the early years of the nineteenth century. He was hanged at Ilchester jail in 1827.

CHECK THE POEM

The anguish of hindsight in a temporal universe – of not being able to go back to change words or actions which have brought unhappiness to others – is a recurrent theme of Hardy. A a similar thematic concern comes to fruition in the *Poems of 1912–13*, with their remorseful recollections of a marriage gone sour, especially perhaps in poems like 'The Going', 'The Voice' and 'After a Journey'.

GLOSSARY

3–4 **to wet ... a nipperkin** to drink (small measures of) alcoholic liquor

5 **ranged** lined up

15 **traps** trappings, belongings

20 **half-a-crown** an English coin (five shillings or 25 pence)

detailed topography, particularly the careful listing of the countryside inns – many of them long since disappeared by the time Hardy wrote the poem – is much more specific than is traditional in **ballads**, and shows Hardy in another mode, that of the historian documenting a vanishing way of life. In this way Hardy places the events recounted in a place that is changing and, very appropriately, in the context of passing time.

As so often in Hardy's poetry, time is a key element in this **tragedy**. In part, of course, the tragedy derives from the terrible consequences of what is really nothing more than foolish behaviour: the outcome is quite disproportionate to the initial actions and, **ironically**, quite the opposite of what the woman intended. But perhaps of greater interest to Hardy is the lifetime's anguish she will suffer because of her thoughtlessness. Even before the sudden death of his wife and the *Poems of 1912–13*, Hardy was aware of the torment of hindsight: if only we had known then what we know now, how differently we would have behaved! Here the woman's final dream-encounter with the ghost of her lover serves only to enhance this bitter recognition.

THE MAN HE KILLED

- A soldier recalls how he killed his enemy as they stood face to face.
- He reflects on the fact that his enemy was a man much like himself, and had they met in a different time or place, he would have offered him a drink.
- The soldier ponders the incomprehensible nature of war.

A soldier says that, had they met in an inn, he might have enjoyed a drink with the man he has killed. However, they found themselves 'ranged' (5) as enemies – and the soldier did his duty when he killed the man. He tries, and fails, to come up with a satisfactory explanation for his action. At the end of the poem, the soldier reiterates his view that he has much in common with the dead man, and would have helped him by offering him money if they had met as civilians.

COMMENTARY

The ironies in this poem are evident from the start. The soldier and the man he killed might have been drinking partners; they were deemed enemies at someone else's bidding and not by choice. They shot at each other as they were ordered to do and the enemy died. The ironies deepen in **stanza** 3 where the speaker struggles to find a good reason for the killing: 'because – / Because he was my foe' (9–10). The conversational style, the hesitation and the repeated 'because' betray his doubt. The **narrator** cannot come up with convincing reasons for the killing – because, the poem makes clear, there aren't any.

In stanza 4 the speaker says that he joined up simply because he was unemployed. And he speculates that his enemy also joined up on impulse for similar reasons ('Was out of work – had sold his traps – ', 15). The soldier's artless confession ('No other reason why', 16) enables the bitter revelation of the poem's deeper meanings: contrary to popular (and comforting) belief, patriotism does not motivate those who fight. The soldier's simplistic conclusion in stanza 5, as he returns to the opening idea of drinking fellowship (and indeed by the possibility of charity) that war is 'quaint and curious' (17), i.e. beyond the comprehension of ordinary mortals, now seems hopelessly inadequate. And the reader is left in no doubt about Hardy's view.

There is an odd discrepancy between the poem itself which is narrated in the first person and the title which employs the third person pronoun 'he'. Thus the reader hears the simple personal testimony – which is the more compelling because of the conversational style (and which is sometimes whimsical: 'off-hand like', 14), and the colloquialism ('to wet / Right many a nipperkin', 3–4) – but is also invited to take a more objective and complex view. This combination of the detached and the intimate tends to universalise the experience described as well as accentuating the ironies. The poem is in plain ballad form, rhyming abab. In fact, the simple **metrical** scheme seems wholly inappropriate for this

CHECK THE POEM

Hardy's war poetry in many ways anticipates the First World War poetry of Wilfred Owen which has the same emphasis on 'the pity of war', and a hatred of jingoism and the glorification of war. Owen's poem 'Strange Meeting' also has an encounter (in Hell) between two dead soldiers, an Englishman and a German, and the latter declares, 'I am the enemy you killed.'

QUESTION

Related by an ordinary soldier, this deceptively simple poem delivers Hardy's own bitter condemnation of the futility of war. In what ways does the ironic effect of the poem depend on the innocence of the speaker?

subject matter, but again it serves the sense of outward simplicity (the voice heard in the poem) concealing a profounder **ironic** meaning.

CHANNEL FIRING

- The noise of gunnery practice out at sea wakes the dead in a country churchyard.
- A cynical God reassures them that this is not the Judgement Day but preparation for war.
- The dead return to their rest reflecting that the world has not improved in their absence.

CHECK THE POEM

Hardy's loss of Christian faith involved a perception that the purveyors of that faith were either ineffectual or even harmful. His antipathy towards clergymen is evident in both novels and poems: consider his portrayal of clergymen in 'The Curate's Kindness' and 'In Church' as well as this poem. The disillusioned Parson Thirdly also appears in *Far From the Madding Crowd* (1874).

The poem, set in a churchyard, is spoken by one of the dead. The noise has shattered windows in the church and the skeletons sit up expectantly thinking it is 'the Judgment-day' (4) (when the final trumpet call will wake the dead and signal the end of creation). God tells them this is not the case but what they hear is the gunnery practice in the English Channel – which shows that nothing has changed in the world since they were buried and countries are just as belligerent as ever. God is bitterly critical of the living: they are 'Mad as hatters' (14) and no more ready to show Christian love (i.e. 'for Christés sake', 15) than are the dead who are of course now 'helpless in such matters' (16). God considers that it is just as well for those preparing for war that it is not the Judgement Day because if it were they would be punished by having to scour the floor of Hell. And God announces that when his Judgement Day comes he will ensure it is hotter than Hell. But he also says he may defer the Day indefinitely on the grounds that what human beings need most is a long rest! The dead reflect on this as they lie down again. They all nod in agreement at the suggestion that human beings are unlikely ever to find alternatives to war as a way of settling their differences.

COMMENTARY

This is a **sardonic** poem, its humour becoming a vehicle for a sharply sarcastic comment on war and religion. There are several sources of black humour: the irreverent portrayal of the dead (for example, Parson Thirdly wishes he had not spent his life sermonising but had 'stuck to pipes and beer', 32), the startled reaction of the animals ('The glebe cow drooled', 9), the wry voice of God (who cracks – and laughs at – a joke of his own about damnation, promises to outdo Hell on Judgement Day but says he may change the date) – and all this ironically delivered in a form reminiscent of a hymn (**iambic tetrameters** rhymed abab).

There seems to be a shift of tone in the last **stanza**, however. Indeed, a darker note may already have been struck in the fourth stanza when God refers to 'All nations striving strong to make / Red war yet redder' (13–14). The apocalyptic **imagery** perhaps betrays Hardy's premonitions about the European political climate. Published just four months before the beginning of the First World War, Hardy would later claim that this poem, with its sense of impending catastrophe, was prophetic. The final lines of the poem remind the reader of the long history of Wessex. What is Hardy suggesting here? Perhaps that nothing has changed since the beginning of time, that human beings have consistently used a religious pretext for killing each other through the ages. Perhaps that God is just as bad as his people. Or even, perhaps, that human beings have created the God that suited their political and territorial ambitions – just as Hardy, in fact, has created a cynical God to suit his own purposes in this poem.

> **CONTEXT**
>
> The place names here are carefully chosen. Stourton Tower commemorates the victory of King Alfred of Wessex over the Danes in AD 879; Camelot was the court of King Arthur, the semi-legendary king of the Britons around the sixth century AD; and Stonehenge is the stone circle near Salisbury, believed to have been in use between 3100 and 1100 BC.

WHEN I SET OUT FOR LYONNESSE

- The poet recalls a journey he made to Lyoness, a place of romance.
- No one could predict what would happen to him when he reached his destination, but when he returns it is clear he has had a life-changing experience.

In the first **stanza** of the poem, the poet describes how he set out on a journey, alone and before dawn; in the second he states that

> **GLOSSARY**
>
> 3 **rime** frost
>
> 3 **spray** small branch bearing flowers, leaves or berries
>
> 7 **bechance** happen
>
> 9 **durst** dared to
>
> 15 **mute surmise** silent conjecture

CHECK THE POEM

This poem was prompted by Hardy's visit in March 1870 to St Juliot, Cornwall, where he met Emma Gifford, who was to become his wife. See 'A Man Was Drawing Near to Me' which tells the story of the meeting from Emma's perspective.

CHECK THE POEM

Lyonnesse is the name for Cornwall in the Arthurian romances of Alfred Tennyson (*Idylls of the King*, 1842–85) who in turn had taken it from Sir Thomas Malory whose *Le Morte Darthur*, telling the story of King Arthur and the Knights of the Round Table, was published in 1485.

GLOSSARY

9 **weird** uncanny, supernatural

neither prophet nor wizard could have predicted what would befall him at his destination, Lyonnesse; and the third describes his return – now a changed man, 'With magic in [his] eyes!' (18).

COMMENTARY

The apparent simplicity of this poem is deceptive. It is a version of a **rondeau**, one of the French verse forms which Hardy experimented with. It does not quite conform to the standard pattern, but the last two lines of each **stanza** repeat the first two, which is the main feature of the rondeau. Here the effect is both to raise the emotional temper of the poem, and to help establish Lyonnesse, or Cornwall, as a landscape of romance. The contrasts between the first and last stanzas draw attention to the transforming nature of the experience which took place there. Initially the **narrator** is 'lit' (4) by the stars, while on his return he is the source of illumination. Similarly, the mundane details (distance, frost) of his departure are replaced by the aura of magic and warmth which he exudes when he returns.

The poem is set entirely in Higher Bockhampton, Dorset, from where Hardy set out on 3 March to travel to St Juliot to supervise the restoration of a church on the instructions of his employer. The poem does not take us to Lyonnesse/Cornwall, but the effect of this reticence is actually to evoke it as an extraordinary place – remote, ideal, timeless and capable of bringing about the magical transformations with which the poem ends. In the later *Poems of 1912–13*, in particular 'After a Journey', 'Beeny Cliff' and 'At Castle Boterel', Hardy, by now an old man, journeys to Cornwall and endeavours to re-enter this landscape of romance in an attempt to recover from memory something of the mood recorded here.

WESSEX HEIGHTS

- The highlands of Wessex provide the poet with an escape from the personal and public disappointments of the 'lowlands' which have brought about an acute personal crisis.
- There is a hint at the end that the highlands may provide a source of spiritual and artistic renewal.

The poet describes how he has ascended the 'Wessex Heights', where he can be alone and free, to escape from the 'lowlands' (5), peopled as they are by the critics of his novels, friends who have fallen out with him and (possibly) women with whom he has had failed relationships. He feels at odds with the world ('nobody thinks as I', 7) – and, in stanza 3, at odds with himself when he imagines his youthful 'simple self' (13) lamenting the man he has become. Hardy wonders whether, after the personal and public pressures which have brought him to this crisis, he will be able to restore mental coherence by wandering the Dorset hills (and, of course, by writing poetry).

COMMENTARY

This poem belongs to a period of crisis and depression in Hardy's life: 1895–6 (see **Background: Thomas Hardy's life**). Significantly, it seems to confirm his abandonment of novel-writing for poetry, and his withdrawal into seclusion in Dorset. The locations of the poem are as much **symbolic** as real: Hardy may be marking out his poetic domain but the contrast between the lowlands (where the novels, particularly *Jude the Obscure*, got him into so much trouble with critics) and the highlands (where he is free to write his poetry) tells us more about his state of mind. There is a pause for bitter reflection in stanza 3, where Hardy says that the 'chrysalis' (16) of his youthful self failed to fulfil its promise. Certainly the 'continuator' (15), that is the middle-aged man who succeeded the youth, proves in the huge **couplets** and leaden (mainly **iambic**) **rhythms** of this poem that, in his depression and lack of will, he is now anything but a butterfly.

The women in this poem have been tentatively identified as Emma Hardy ('the lone man's friend' in stanza 2), Hardy's mother (the 'figure' in stanza 4), Tryphena Sparks (all three ghosts in stanza 5) and Mrs Henniker ('one rare fair woman' in stanza 6). Perhaps the most noteworthy thing about them is their ghostliness: here, Hardy wants to keep the 'ghosts' at 'their distance' (32) – it is a measure of his depression and **alienation** – but in later poems he will actively seek to re-engage with them and his past.

CHECK THE POEM

Hardy's reference to the 'mind-chains' (8) of the lowlands is reminiscent of the 'mind-forged manacles' in William Blake's famous poem 'London' (1792). Here Blake attacks the stifling influence of conventional opinion.

CONTEXT

In December 1914, Florence, Hardy's second wife, wrote in a letter to a friend: 'the four people mentioned are actual women. One was dead & three living when it was written [1896] – now only one is living … "Wessex Heights" will always wring my heart, for I know when it was written a little while after the publication of "Jude", when he was so cruelly treated'.

UNDER THE WATERFALL

UNDER THE WATERFALL

GLOSSARY

9 **purl** rippling flow

10 **span** distance between tips of thumb and little finger, 23 cm

24 **opalized** rendered iridescent (like the gemstone opal) by the action of the water

40 **throe** a violent pang; a spasm of feeling

47 **lours** darkens

48 **chalice** goblet

CONTEXT

In her memoir *Some Recollections*, Emma Hardy says: 'often we walked down the beautiful [Vallency] Valley to Boscastle harbour where we had to jump over stones and climb over a low wall by rough steps, to come out on great wide spaces suddenly, with a sparkling little brook into which we once lost a tiny picnic tumbler'. At the time Hardy sketched Emma searching for the glass; many years later, he wrote this poem.

- A woman recalls a picnic by a waterfall when she dropped a drinking-glass into the water and neither she nor her lover could retrieve it.
- She experiences anew the romantic emotions she felt on that day whenever she dips her arm into a basin of water.

A woman is imagined recounting the incident of losing a glass in a waterfall on a romantic picnic with her future husband. Ever since, placing her hand in water brings back the 'sweet sharp sense' (3) of that day. But the romantic memory is undercut by a sense of loss and the second more sceptical voice we hear.

COMMENTARY

Written in the knowledge that the relationship between Emma and Thomas had deteriorated, this poem scrutinises the myth of eternal love, making it a fitting prelude to the *Poems of 1912–13*.

The poem subverts its **lyrical** and idyllic surface in a variety of ways. The central event of the poem is a fall – of the drinking glass into the water, and its loss. And the **motif** of falling runs through the poem: the waterfall, the passing years conceived as falling curtain (this is a memory of 'a fugitive day, / Fetched back from its thickening shroud of gray', 3–4), and a fall from innocence (the romance of the young lovers on that August day, never to be repeated). The woman is reminded of that special day whenever she dips her arm into a basin of water which is a kind of fall from the authenticity of the original experience. There are other unsettling notes: the trite **couplets** in lines 5–8 and lines 25–8, the less than lyrical 'hollow boiling voice' (15) of the brook, and the sceptical second voice which does not seem to share the woman's enthusiasm for the myths of love. In fact, the accumulative effect of all these jarring notes would seem to suggest that the outcome here was not eternal love – that, indeed, the relationship itself 'fell.'

The poem does not deny that a mundane action in the present can prompt a recovery of deep feeling about a past event – or indeed that human beings desire this kind of magical experience. But it does invite us to look again at the phenomenon. Is the experience valid? Is it a fiction to think we can recover the past? Are our responses conditioned by cultural myths (of love, in this case)? Here all these questions are implicit in the second more realist voice – and the woman's sentimentality about love is challenged. But she is not dissuaded: she tells the story, and the poem concludes with an act of imagination in which she asserts the meaning of the glass as a **symbol** of true love. But, as is the case earlier in the poem, the discordant notes remain, and the processes of time and change are remorseless: the glass is lost, 'Jammed darkly, nothing to show how prized' (23), and altered in appearance by the action of the water, 'its smoothness opalized' (24).

The poem comprises a series of irregular couplets. At this stage of his poetry writing Hardy was experimenting with irregular **stanza**-forms. It has been suggested, unconvincingly perhaps, that the stanza-shapes suggest a waterfall. Nevertheless, it is evident in the poem that Hardy employs **onomatopoeic diction** and rapid **rhythms** in order to mimic the motion and sound of the waterfall in lines 13–16.

FROM *POEMS OF 1912–13*

The following poems (from 'The Going' to 'Places') are from the famous sequence of **elegies** that Hardy wrote following the death of his wife Emma. You can find a critical overview of the sequence in **Critical approaches**. The Latin **epigraph** 'Veteris vestigia flammae' is taken from Virgil's **epic** *Aeneid* (first century BC) and means 'traces of the old flame'.

CHECK THE POEM

In the poem 'On a Midsummer Eve' – a time of enchantment – Hardy recalls dipping his hand into a brook which seemed to conjure up the ghost of Emma, suggesting perhaps that this was a key motif in his recollections of his courtship.

CHECK THE POEM

'At Castle Boterel' (see **Extended commentaries**) and 'Where the Picnic Was' are also poems from the 1912–13 sequence.

THE GOING

THE GOING

* Emma's sudden death has caught Hardy by surprise and left him distraught.
* He remembers their idyllic courtship, when Emma was young and beautiful, and contrasts it with their more recent estrangement.

GLOSSARY

9 **lip me** give voice to (with suggestions perhaps of a ghostly kiss)

25 **beetling** projecting, overhanging

CONTEXT

There has been much biographical debate on the extent to which Hardy knew how serious Emma's condition was. Robert Gittings (*The Older Hardy*, 1978) says she had been very ill and he ignored it. If this is true, then Emma's death really brought home to him his neglect of her and this could explain the depths of his remorse. Contrastingly, however, Claire Tomalin (*Thomas Hardy*, 2007) suggests Emma's affliction was long-standing and her sudden death was therefore a great surprise to Hardy.

This is Hardy's first attempt to come to terms with the shock of Emma's death, which has reawakened all his old feelings for her. Hardy asks his wife why she gave 'no hint' (1) of her imminent death, which has 'altered all' (14). He recalls the days of their courtship – and then we learn that his anguish is sharpened by the lack of communication in the latter years of their relationship. But nothing can be changed now – and she will never know how her death has affected him.

COMMENTARY

The striking aspect of this poem's tone is the way it shifts backwards and forwards between remorse and irritation. Alongside the grief at Emma's death, we hear echoes of the couple's marital squabbling. 'Why did you give no hint' (1), he chides her from the start. This bitterness is perhaps at its most chilling in the second **stanza**: the reiterated complaint that she slipped away without a word of farewell ('Never to bid good-bye / Or lip me the softest call', 8–9) almost seems to suggest that she died to spite him, to get her own back for his harshness towards her, which lasted until the moment of her death (as the rather odd use of the word 'harden' to describe the daylight in line 11 reminds us). But there are other ways in which Emma's 'great going … altered all' (13–14) and any bitterness is offset by his sadness – the difficult realisation that he will never see her again, the agony of his reviving love for her, and his feelings of emptiness.

Hardy's anguish is superbly conveyed at the close of stanza 3, when for a moment ('a breath', 16) he thinks he sees her strolling, as used to be the case, between the trees at dusk: 'Till in darkening dankness / The yawning blankness / Of the perspective sickens me!' (19–21) Following this we learn of the way their relationship deteriorated. In stanza 4 there is a glimpse of Emma as she was at the time of their idyllic courtship in Cornwall: the 'red-veined rocks' (23), with their fleshy overtones, are associated with her and suggest how she was then full of youth, life and vigour and completely at one with that romantic landscape. Stanza 5 returns to the present and we realise that the note of irritation in the poem probably derives from self-reproach: in addition to the sorrow at her passing there are feelings of guilt, for both the animosity of recent years and, latterly, the neglect of her suffering. As a consequence the poem's tone modulates, after all, into forgiveness and tenderness – although the faltering **rhythms** and broken **syntax** of the final stanza betray the despair which undercuts this.

In view of the title, it is revealing to examine the various uses of the verb 'to go' in this poem – in the various senses of leaving ('be gone', 4), dying ('great going', 13) and letting things go ('It must go', 37) – since they help plot the progress of Hardy's pain and serve to invest Emma with unique qualities. They certainly underline the notion of movement and travelling which is characteristic of the whole sequence of the *Poems of 1912–13*. This perhaps denotes travelling *in time*, which is the lot of human beings and a source of sorrow in this poem and elsewhere in Hardy's work – a view of life as a journey subject to time and change. Hardy is perhaps lamenting the impossibility of revisiting the past to change things in the light of new awareness, specifically here the realisation of Emma's centrality to the plot (as Hardy saw it) of his life. In later poems in the sequence Hardy will attempt the difficult task of travelling back in time in an attempt to reclaim the past, even if he cannot 'amend' (36) it.

Some critics have found the form of the poem to run counter to its emotions – a **metrical** 'box' into which Hardy has had to force his meaning. The problem really centres on lines 5 and 6 of each stanza: unlike the other lines, which tend to echo the rhythms of speech, these **iambic dimeter couplets** with **feminine endings** could sound incongruously light and tripping. This is perfectly acceptable in stanza 4 – where the context (the ecstatic courtship days) justifies

CHECK THE POEM

Tennyson's *In Memoriam* (1833–50) is a model for the *Poems of 1912–13*. A more immediate influence was Coventry Patmore's sequence *To the Unknown Eros*, addressed to his dead wife. In 'Departure', Patmore asks: 'Do you … / Never … repent / Of how, that June afternoon, / You went, / With sudden, unintelligible phrase, And frightened eye, / Upon your journey of so many days, / Without a single kiss, or a good-bye?'

CHECK THE BOOK

Donald Davie, in *Thomas Hardy and British Poetry* (1972), writes: 'the imperious verbal engineer still, even here, thwarting the true and truly suffering poet'.

QUESTION

Do form and meaning contradict each other in this poem – or does the form enable a more complex interpretation?

the tone – but is more surprising elsewhere (e.g. 'Where I could not follow / With wing of swallow', 5–6). One could argue that the abrupt change of tone in fact sharpens the poignancy of the poem. Alternatively, it has been suggested that the heavy **stresses** in these lines actually work against the insubstantial **rhymes**. Perhaps Hardy wishes to emphasise that, contrary to what many may think, poetry in fact offers no simple consolation, or therapy, to those suffering real emotional torment.

YOUR LAST DRIVE

- Hardy recalls what was to be Emma's last drive when she passed the graveyard where she would be buried only eight days later.
- Hardy could have seen no hint in Emma's face that she would shortly be oblivious to all that her husband might say or do.
- He declares that, nevertheless, he will not neglect her now.

CHECK THE BOOK

Hardy believed that experience could be written on the brain, on the face or on the landscape. Here he says that he could not have read the writing on Emma's face that night. Similarly, Clym Yeobright's face in Book 3, Ch. 1 of *The Return of the Native* (1878) has his experience written on it: 'The observer's eye was arrested, not by his face as a picture, but by his face as a page; not by what it was, but by what it recorded.'

Hardy continues to register his shock at Emma's sudden death. This is a calmer poem than 'The Going' and is sometimes seen as a prelude to recovery. The balance has shifted more towards sympathy for Emma, but Hardy's self-reproach is also explicit. He reflects that Emma had no idea, on what was to prove to be her last drive, that she would never again see the 'borough lights' (2) (of Dorchester); nor, as she passed the churchyard (of Stinsford), that she would shortly be laid to rest there forever. Hardy imagines that the future was written on Emma's face that evening if he had been able to read it: soon she would be dead, oblivious to everything, not knowing whether he misses her, whether he visits her grave or not, or whether he speaks well of her or not (and there is a clear reproach here for the harsh words he spoke to her while she lived). But equally she will never know, as his assertion that he will not neglect her now she is gone makes clear, that his former love for her has been reawakened.

COMMENTARY

Although the tensions evident in 'The Going' are still present, Hardy now seems to feel more tenderness than animosity towards

Emma. **Ironically**, now that she is dead he is 'closer' to her than he has been for years. He calls her 'Dear ghost' (27) – the odd **juxtaposition** suggesting why the pain is so intense. The unassailable fact of her death is effectively communicated in the reference to the 'flickering sheen' (16) of Emma's face on that last drive: she was so recently infused with life, but now that mysterious spark has been extinguished and she is a corpse. Moreover, the word 'flickering' is ambiguous, carrying suggestions of transience, which in this context hints at premonition.

Hardy doesn't spare himself in this poem. He says that even if he had been with Emma on that last drive, he would have failed to notice 'the writing upon [her] face' (17). He does not, of course, mean that her fate was inscribed on her face – but in a sense that *his* fate was. If only he had had the wit to anticipate how he might feel upon Emma's death, if only he had treated her better while she was alive. 'If only …' he had known then what he knows now he would have avoided all this anguish and guilt. Having been drawn into a dialogue with Emma's ghost – and the illusion that it is still possible to seek Emma's forgiveness – he finally accepts the reality of the situation, and the poem ends with a bleakly despairing **couplet**:

> Yet abides the fact, indeed, the same, –
> You are past love, praise, indifference, blame. (29–30)

 QUESTION

What is the effect of the final word of this poem – 'blame' (30) – on its message and tone?

THE WALK

- Hardy recalls how Emma was too weak to go on walks with him at the end of her life.
- Walking alone is nevertheless quite a different experience for him now that Emma is dead.

Hardy is still preoccupied with the suddenness of Emma's death but it is more difficult to judge his mood in this poem. The 'difference' (14) between then (when she was alive) and now (that she is dead) is starkly evoked here. Hardy describes his habitual walk, often taken alone recently because of Emma's illness. He has taken the same walk again since her death but now he is 'alone' (7) in a quite different sense and he tries to define what that difference is.

COMMENTARY

Again, Hardy uses the idea of a journey. His walk is both real – the actual route which he was accustomed to take – and **metaphorical** – that space of time during which Emma died and things were never the same again. The poem is carefully structured to suggest an outward journey, leaving behind a familiar setting, and a return to a room which is the same yet not the same – a room with an absence, an emptiness. That is the 'difference' (14).

In this poem, any impulse to blame Emma has gone. There doesn't seem to be any self-reproach here either. These absences, together with the orderliness of the poem and its restraint, are often interpreted as evidence that Hardy has achieved a measure of calm, a further stage in his recovery. But the very same features could also be seen as evidence of the despair which follows shock in traditional **elegy**. The reality of Hardy's anguish, whatever the outward (poetic) appearance, can perhaps be judged by the change of **rhythm** in the final terse **couplet** – that is, the forced pause after 'sense' (15) and the largely **anapaestic** final line (when earlier long lines have been mainly **iambic**). Certainly this is a return with a 'difference', both **metrically** and emotionally.

QUESTION

R. P. Blackmur (in an essay for *The Southern Review*, 1940) says of this poem: 'it is a style reduced to anonymity, reduced to riches'. It is certainly true that Hardy tells us so little in this poem that it is difficult to judge his mood. But does the very economy of expression enable us to resolve this issue?

GLOSSARY

14 **loamy cell** grave

22 **Dundagel** Tintagel (associated with King Arthur)

26 **Lyonnesse** north-west Cornwall (see 'When I Set Out for Lyonnesse')

38 **domiciled** lived

I FOUND HER OUT THERE

- The poet reflects on the fact that Emma is buried far from the wild Cornish coast that defined her youthful self, and was where they met.
- He imagines her ghost being drawn back towards the ocean she loved.

The poem describes how Hardy met Emma in Cornwall (the life-changing event in 'When I Set Out for Lyonnesse') and then brought her back to Dorset, where she now lies buried. He reflects that she is far from the country she loved, the space of her youth, her vitality and her dreams. He imagines her ghost stealing westwards to hear again the sound of the Atlantic waves which once gave her so much joy (in 'My Spirit Will Not Haunt the Mound' a ghostly Emma reveals a similar intention). And the poem anticipates the pilgrimage Hardy will himself make in later poems to the scenes of his courtship of Emma. Cornwall is again seen as a landscape of romance and Emma a figure who properly belongs there.

COMMENTARY

The poem's effectiveness lies in its use of contrasts. The reality of Dorset, where Emma lies buried, is contrasted with Cornwall, that place of romance which is far away. This is also a contrast of time, of course: *then*, when Emma was young and full of life, and *now*, when she is a corpse. Cornwall is a place of wind and crashing breakers, while Emma's Dorset grave is 'noiseless' (11); Cornwall was a place of freedom for Emma, but now she lies in her 'loamy cell' (14). And the point is of course that she was fully at home in Cornwall, and partook of its natural characteristics. Thus, for example, the sun 'Dyed her face fire-red' (24) there, implicitly drawing attention to her sexual vitality.

This poem seems less concerned with expressing Hardy's pain at his bereavement (although it is present, as is the continuing note of self-reproach) than with trying to capture the essence of Emma. The poem concludes with an **image** of rebirth characteristic of the elegy: Emma's ghost hears the Atlantic waves and is resurrected 'With the heart of a child' (40), a quality which was uniquely hers. Finally, part of the picturing of Emma in this poem depends on the representation of Cornwall as a landscape of romance. Its remoteness and wildness are stressed, but more subtly it is seen as a place of stories and legends: its cliffs are 'haunted' (18), Dundagel head is 'famed' (22), and, poignantly, Emma herself 'would sigh at the tale / Of sunk Lyonnesse' (25–6). But just as the myths of Lyonnesse belong to a fabled past, so too does the love story of Emma and Thomas Hardy – for it was engendered in that romantic place but later fell victim to the realities of time and circumstance.

CONTEXT

Hardy drew on Emma's account of their meeting in *Some Recollections* for this poem. The meeting was fictionalised by Hardy in the novel *A Pair of Blue Eyes* (1873). The description of the meeting in lines 1–8 here explains the change which comes over Hardy between the first and last stanzas in 'When I Set Out for Lyonnesse' and echoes the romantic mood of the earlier poem.

 CHECK THE POEM

Images of rebirth are characteristic of elegy but there may be an echo here of Wordsworth's 'Lucy' poems (all of which appeared in *Lyrical Ballads*, 1800), and 'I Travelled Among Unknown Men' (1807). These poems express loneliness and loss and celebrate an idealised woman.

WITHOUT CEREMONY

- Hardy reflects on Emma's way of going off on her own and not saying goodbye – which was also true of her death.

? QUESTION

Hardy sometimes addresses Emma as 'you' in these poems and sometimes as 'her'. In 'Without Ceremony', after the indirect address ('her') of the previous poem, he returns to the direct address ('you') employed in the first three poems of the sequence. But here the 'you' is much gentler than in the earlier poems. Why is this so and how does it affect your understanding of the poem?

After the experiments with more conventional **elegy,** Hardy returns to the manner of the opening poems of the sequence. However, he seems to have moved beyond shock at Emma's death. Hardy recalls that she had a habit – after friends had visited, when planning an excursion to town – of slipping off without a word. This was the manner of her death, too, which makes him wonder whether this behaviour betokened more than a belief that saying goodbye was unnecessary. Was it, rather, an implied criticism of his treatment of her in the latter years of their marriage?

COMMENTARY

There is no suggestion of apportioning blame here: Hardy's attitude towards Emma – who he calls 'my dear' (1) – seems to be tender throughout. He does not invoke any of the **motifs** of conventional elegy here. Indeed, this is a strikingly matter-of-fact poem compared with 'I Found Her Out There'. The deliberately unpoetical qualities of the writing – the **rhythms** of speech, the everyday **diction**, the absence of **imagery**, the understated patterning of the poem (notice how the **rhymes** of the first lines in each **stanza** are limited) – all contribute to a kind of poignant domestication of Emma's death. Hardy's self-reproach is related to this process. He now realises that his inference that she couldn't be bothered to say 'Goodbye' was wrong; rather, it was the consequence of his animosity towards her. The poem quietly affirms the importance of saying 'Goodbye', but it is too late to change anything now.

In emotional terms, the poem is strikingly restrained. Hardy's style is characteristically reticent, but even by his standards this poem is remarkably spare. Perhaps what the poem doesn't say is more important than what it does. Is there a grudgingly painful realisation that his inference was wrong? More generally, the tone of the poem is finally balanced between resignation and despair.

THE HAUNTER

- Emma's ghost lovingly haunts Hardy.
- She recalls past joys and recent problems in their relationship – but, aware that Hardy again loves her as he used to, she promises to help restore his peace of mind.

Emma's ghost can be neither seen nor heard by Hardy but she is with him constantly, responding to the desolate appeals of the earlier poems. She reflects on the changes in their relationship – the early shared love of nature and old churches, the later estrangement – and the way her death has revived his love for her. She hopes that her ghostly presence may save him from despair and give him the will to go on living. This poem amounts to wish-fulfilment but it seems appropriate at this stage of the sequence.

COMMENTARY

For the first time in the *Poems of 1912–13*, Hardy gives a voice to Emma's ghost. He imagines her saying all the things he longs to hear. That this is a complete fiction is underlined by the fact that Hardy cannot hear her: she addresses the reader and we are urged to 'tell him' (25) that she is a benign ghost who wishes to heal him with her love and fidelity. This raises the whole question of the sense in which Hardy can be said to 'hear' the dead Emma's voice at all, which will be taken up again in the next poem, 'The Voice'. Here, the fact that this is a fantasy sharpens the reader's sense of Hardy's desolation: if only he *could* hear her! But that would be a scenario of romance and not reality, which the **ballad**-like echoes of this poem **ironically** hint at.

Finally, the representation of Emma's ghost in this poem is problematic. She seems remarkably forgiving. Or is it simply that the impulse to view her wholly sympathetically (after the earlier

 QUESTION

In what ways does the ghost of the older Emma ('The Haunter') differ from the ghost of the younger Emma ('After a Journey' and 'At Castle Boterel')? Does the poet view these two versions of Emma's ghost differently?

 CHECK THE POEM

This poem is a **dramatic monologue** like 'In a Eweleaze near Weatherbury', 'The Man He Killed', 'My Spirit Will Not Haunt the Mound' and 'A Man Was Drawing Near to Me'.

irritation) has now developed? In the second **stanza** she touches on the central **irony** of the whole sequence: that Hardy wants her more now than he did when she was alive. But she is very even-tempered about this, showing little sense of reproach. And, by implication, Hardy acknowledges his wife's finer qualities here – but ultimately this cannot alleviate his guilt: Emma is dead, and communication between them fails here as it did when she was alive.

THE VOICE

- Hardy imagines that he hears Emma's ghostly voice calling him saying that she is once again the young woman he courted.
- Then, in a despairing moment of loneliness and grief, he wonders whether it is simply the breeze he hears.

 CHECK THE POEM

Compare 'Two in the Campagna' (in *Men and Women*, 1855) by Robert Browning (a poet Hardy admired), which contains the line, 'I would that you were all to me'. Browning's poem explores the fleeting nature of love; it also raises the difficulty of finding the right words to communicate living human experience. Hardy was himself well aware that poetry could only offer an approximation to reality (an issue he raises, for example, in 'A Circular' and 'The Last Signal').

Hardy hears Emma's voice calling him, saying that she has reverted to her earlier self which he loved so much. But is it really her he hears? If so, he says he wants to see her as she was in Cornwall in the earliest days of their courtship. But already his confidence that he *can* hear her has gone. Perhaps, after all, it was only the sound of the breeze. Emma is gone forever and he is a desolate old man. This is perhaps the bleakest of all the poems in the sequence. **Paradoxically**, though, it does mark a real turning point after the earlier false starts: following this Hardy begins the process of recovery, and soon will make the trip to Cornwall where he met and fell in love with Emma over forty years ago.

COMMENTARY

This poem further explores the issue raised in the previous poem. Can Hardy hear his wife's voice or not? The poem is constructed to register his growing doubts about this: the relative excitement of the first two stanzas gives way to the growing uncertainty of the third and the bleakness of the fourth. In fact, the doubts are already present in the second stanza: Hardy recalls Emma waiting to meet him in her 'air-blue gown' (8), an unusual **compound epithet** which perhaps does communicate her youthful vitality, but more poignantly suggests that this particular ghost already has the potential to disappear. And this is what happens in the third stanza, where the vision fades: the voice modulates into the breeze, and the ghost dissolves to 'wan wistlessness' (11) – that is, becomes pale (ghostly) and, paradoxically, both wistful and unwitting. In the final stanza Hardy writes that the woman is still 'calling' (16), not now because he expects to actually hear her, but in order to express the unbearable longing for her which he will feel until he himself dies.

The **metrical** effects of this poem are striking. The voice of the woman coming and going on the breeze ('is it only the breeze[?]', 9) is suggested by the **dactylic tetrameters** employed in the first three stanzas, the **triple rhymes** (e.g. 'call to me', 'all to me') on lines 1 and 3, and the abrupt truncation (they are two syllables short) of the other two lines. In the final irregular stanza the metre breaks down completely: basically **trochaic**, there are three **stresses** in lines 13 and 14, four in line 15, and possibly only two (depending on how it is read) in the final line. In effect the **rhythm** stumbles, emulating the 'faltering' (13) steps of the aged speaker as his hopes of seeing his phantom-wife are dashed.

The landscape is also used to enhance Hardy's emotional desolation at the end of this poem. The vision of youthful Emma in her summery attire forty-two years before fades, and Hardy again sees before him the dead winter landscape of present reality. '[L]istlessness' (9) is the key word here, ostensibly describing the breeze, but more applicable to Hardy's state of mind at the end of the poem, after the earlier – but momentary – respite. The emphasis on the effects of change and decay in nature serves to remind us of the same processes at work in human experience: 'Leaves around me falling, / Wind oozing thin through the thorn from norward' (14–15). The falling rhythms (dactyls and trochees) of the poem's penultimate line vividly evoke Hardy's downward spiral into the despair of the final line, where – now in his mind only – the woman is still 'calling' (16).

Conversely, however, a closer look suggests that there is also something more positive going on in the poem. There are glimpses of the young Emma of their courtship days, and an attempt to

 QUESTION

There are some interesting uses of language in this poem – for example, the word 'wistlessness' (11) which is a coinage, or **neologism**; and the echo-like repetition 'how you call to me, call to me' (1). What effect do these language choices have on the poem?

displace the more recent version of her. The poem seems to present Hardy at his lowest point, but it contains the seeds of recovery (however ambivalent that recovery might prove to be). The process we see here is developed in later poems with the pilgrimage to Cornwall and the reclaiming of an idyllic past.

A CIRCULAR

- Hardy opens a letter addressed to Emma containing a fashion brochure.
- Sardonically, Hardy points out that her last outfit was the shroud she was buried in.

CHECK THE BOOK

Hardy showed a recurring interest in failed communications. Often this was because of his understanding of the imperfect nature of language, but sometimes it was simply his perception of the wry irony of things – as, for example, the letter confessing her sexual past which Tess writes to Angel Clare before their marriage in *Tess of the d'Urbervilles* (1891) and which he does not see because it becomes lodged under the carpet – a piece of bad luck which results in Angel abandoning her.

Hardy, as Emma's 'legal representative' (1), opens her post and finds a brochure for ladies' spring fashion. But the lady for whom it was meant was buried last winter, 'costumed in a shroud' (12). This poem might almost be seen as an **ironic** comment on the whole sequence of the *Poems of 1912–13* which are, similarly, messages which will never be delivered as the intended recipient is dead.

COMMENTARY

In some ways this short poem typifies Hardy's outlook on life: he attaches great significance to moments like this and seems to derive, as the final line suggests, a grim pleasure from them.

In formal terms, the poem attempts to catch something of the stilted, formulaic **diction** of the brochure ('in tints as shown', 'Warranted up to date', 4, 8). In fact, Emma is as dead as the language in the brochure. Perhaps Hardy is quietly expressing an anxiety of his own – that words may betray the dead, and Emma in particular, by failing to capture the essential life that was once theirs (see the 'flickering sheen', 16, in Emma's face mentioned in 'Your Last Drive'). If we see the *Poems of 1912–13* as a chronological sequence, documenting Hardy's journey through his grief and guilt, the desire to recapture Emma may appear a particularly relevant concern to him, as he prepares for the pilgrimage to Cornwall and his poetic envisioning of his lost wife at the time of their courtship.

AFTER A JOURNEY

- Hardy tracks the ghost of the youthful Emma in her old Cornish haunts.
- He wonders whether she has thought about the way the early promise of their relationship in these very locations went unfulfilled – and ended in bitterness and recrimination.
- The ghost will disappear with the breaking dawn, but Hardy, hoping to encounter her again, asserts that he has not changed since those romantic days many years ago.

The poems set in Cornwall – in particular this one, 'Beeny Cliff' and 'At Castle Boterel' – form the core of the 1912–13 sequence. The issue at stake in all three is the effort to reclaim the past as a way of resisting the processes of time and change. Here, Hardy follows the ghost of the youthful Emma to the scenes of their courtship in Cornwall forty-three years before. Has she reflected on the way their relationship deteriorated after its idyllic beginnings? That cannot be changed, however, and the implication therefore is that this return to the past might offer some comfort. Hardy urges the ghost to bring him again to these locations as he claims he is 'just the same' (31) as he was all those years ago.

COMMENTARY

This is a stunning poem – some readers would say the central poem of the sequence (though 'At Castle Boterel' also has a claim to this status). What is so impressive here is the effort of consciousness, of memory and language, to challenge the brute facts of the material world: on the one hand, the processes of time and change (the passage from summer to autumn defines the decay of the relationship in **stanza** 2 – 'Summer gave us sweets, but autumn wrought division', 13); and on the other, an indifferent universe (the

GLOSSARY

29 **lours** looks sullen

CHECK THE BOOK

Traditionally ghosts disappear at dawn, as, for example, does the ghost of Claudius in the first scene of Shakespeare's *Hamlet*.

QUESTION

In an essay entitled 'The Modernity of Hardy's Poetry' (in *The Cambridge Companion to Thomas Hardy*, ed. Dale Kramer, 1999), John Paul Riquelme says that 'After a Journey' is 'a poem about repetitions with a difference, both repetitions that create something new and ones that cannot recapture a lost original'. In this respect the echoing cave becomes a central **motif** of the poem. What repetitions can you identify in the poem and what do they signify?

CHECK THE BOOK

In *Thomas Hardy and British Poetry* (1972), Donald Davie offers a positive interpretation of the poem which, he says, ends with 'unprecedented serenity'.

physical presence of the landscape is striking in this and the other core poems – for example, the **onomatopoeic** qualities of the 'unseen waters' ejaculations', 4). The poem wishes to assert that the human mind, which understands loss, lack and insignificance, is also capable of reclaiming the past and imposing human value on the landscape. In Hardy's mind the waterfall, and the cave (which 'seems to call out to me from forty years ago', 22), will always be associated with Emma and with those romantic events which took place many years before but which are vividly present both in memory and landscape 'now' (24).

But how successful in fact is Hardy in reclaiming the past here, and in defeating time? Some critics say that the vividness with which Emma is imagined confirms that love has indeed triumphed over time in this poem. This view is problematic, however. Hardy *almost* captures Emma in **stanza** 1 (denoted by the description of her here – 'With your nut-coloured hair, / And gray eyes, and rose-flush coming and going', 7–8) but she remains elusive. By the third stanza, even though the memory is briefly vivid, Emma is reduced to a 'thin ghost' (24) and Hardy is left only with the mocking echo from the cave (suggested by the **feminine rhymes** and **alliteration** on 'l': 'hollow', 'call', 'all aglow', 'frailly follow'). Throughout there is the curious sense that Hardy is talking not to Emma but to himself. This is because he cannot forget that she is actually dead and that before her death he was on very bad terms with her. This is especially evident in stanza 2, where the sombre tone is as much a product of the **diction** ('years', 'dead scenes', 'past', 'dark space', 'lacked', 'division' – and the ambiguity of 'twain', not simply 'two' but 'divided') as of the **rhythms**. Indeed, the last line seems to suggest that time holds the upper hand here. So this first attempt to envision the youthful Emma (Hardy says he has come here in order to 'view a voiceless ghost', 1, having renounced all hope of dialogue with her), to reclaim the past, and to assert a love which might defeat time, ends not in serenity but in disappointment and bitterness. This is confirmed in the final stanza: an indifferent nature offers no comfort, and daylight erases the last possibility of vision (the ghost returns to the grave). It has been suggested that the final lines of this poem show the triumph of conviction (and therefore of vision) over the realities of time and change. But perhaps the jarring rhyme ('lours'/'flowers', 29, 32) undermines Hardy's assertion that he is 'just the same' (31) as he was in those far-off, idyllic days. As a consequence the poem ends, in fact, on a note of despair.

BEENY CLIFF

- Hardy recalls Emma riding on Beeny Cliff.
- Years later, Beeny Cliff still stands but Emma is dead and the joys of their courtship just a memory.

Hardy vividly recalls the time he visited Beeny Cliff with Emma forty-three years ago. It provided a beautiful backdrop to their courtship, part of the idyllic quality of the day (they hardly noticed the changing weather). But he now stands there alone and the cliff seems a more ominous presence. Whatever memories it holds for him, the reality is that Emma is dead and it means nothing to her. Here, Hardy seems more reconciled to the processes of time which have brought about these changes.

COMMENTARY

Each stanza is self-contained but, with the third stanza as a pivot, the poem contrasts 'then' and 'now', as do many of the *Poems of 1912–13*. The first two stanzas recall the scene in 1870 through both sight and sound. The opening line is striking: 'O the opal and the sapphire of that wandering western sea'. Here the long, rhythmic line, the description of the colours of the sea in terms of jewels and the unusual use of 'wandering' to portray its movement are very effective. The tone set is one of exhilaration, and thereafter the lovers – Emma in particular – are vividly evoked. The scene changes in stanza 3. There is a shower, and the Atlantic is briefly overcast. The lovers seem oblivious to this slightly darker note, but it provides a transition to stanzas 4 and 5 – away from memory (however reluctantly) and into the sadness of the present. The shift is marked by the changed aspect of the landscape: the cliff retains its 'chasmal beauty' (10) but in stanza 4 it 'bulks' (10) and in stanza 5 it 'looms' (13). Nevertheless, in Hardy's thoughts it seems to take

 CHECK THE POEM

In his diary for 10 March 1870, Hardy wrote: 'Went with E.L.G. to Beeny Cliff. She on horseback ... On the cliff ... "The tender grace of a day", etc.' The reference is to Tennyson's poem 'Break, break, break' (in *English Idylls*, 1842) – a **lament** for his friend Arthur Hallam. The poem continues: 'The tender grace of a day that is dead / Will never come back to me'. It is **ironic** that Hardy suppressed this final line in his diary entry. The opening line of 'Beeny Cliff' is very Tennysonian in style.

second place to the fact that 'The woman now is – elsewhere –' (14), the hesitation communicating all the more effectively the painful recognition that Emma is dead.

The stanza form is unusual – **iambic** (for the most part) **heptameters** with **rhymes** in triplets. But it is the facility with which Hardy manipulates the **rhythms**, often in conjunction with **alliteration**, within this framework that is impressive. In the first two **stanzas** in particular, the long, fluid lines with their effortlessly modulating rhythms generate a sense of excitement and identification between the lovers and the landscape on that day long ago. The alliteration on 'l' in line 6 clinches this: 'laughed light-heartedly aloft'. Alliteration on 'd' and 'l' in stanza 3 adds an ominous dimension to what is only a passing rain-cloud which temporarily darkens the ocean, but which as a consequence casts a shadow over the rest of the poem: 'And the Atlantic dyed its levels with a dull misfeatured stain' (8). Stanza 4 opens with a pause denoting a transition to the realities of the present and a change to slower, less flexible rhythms. This is immediately confirmed by the alliteration on 'b' in line 10, which now endows the cliff where the lovers once frolicked with a sinister aspect: 'Still in all its chasmal beauty bulks old Beeny to the sky'. After the opulence of earlier lines, the monosyllables which enunciate the questions of lines 11 and 12 bring out Hardy's despair. In stanza 5, strong and meaningful pauses frame the word 'elsewhere'. The final line, with its heavy rhythm and hollow, echoing sounds, seems drained of hope.

There is an unspoken question at the end of the poem. Where is Emma now? In effect this is the question that all the core poems of the sequence ask. Here, the answer seems to be that she exists in Hardy's memory, forever associated with the sites of their courtship. Unlike 'After a Journey', there is no pretence that time can be defeated. The 'resurrection' of Emma in the opening stanzas is counterbalanced by the recognition later that she is, in reality, dead.

In this poem Hardy gives equal weight to vivid memory and present reality. But it is perhaps worth noting that in order to achieve this

CHECK THE BOOK

In response to the question 'Where is Emma now?' Donald Davie (in *Thomas Hardy and British Poetry*, 1972) says that in this poem (and in 'After a Journey' and 'At Castle Boterel') Emma has become a spirit who will haunt forever the natural sites she inhabited when Hardy first loved her – which, he adds, is a surprising assertion for Hardy, an agnostic and a humanist.

balance, Hardy has resorted to a significant omission. Nothing is allowed to compromise the representation of the blissful lovers. Drawing on the conventions of romance, the poem asserts that all they had to fear was time and death. And to do this, as readers of the preceding poems know, Hardy has had to quietly suppress the truth about the deterioration of his subsequent relationship with Emma.

PLACES

- Scenes from Emma's childhood and youth are lost to all but Hardy, but he values them more than the present.

Previous poems in the sequence had sought to recover the youthful Emma in Cornwall. Here, for the first two 'places', Hardy also casts his mind further back to her childhood in Plymouth, Devon. No one, he says, thinks of Emma's birth in Plymouth over seventy years ago; no one thinks of the little girl lying in bed listening to the nearby church bells; and no one thinks of the young woman riding recklessly over the hill near her new home in Cornwall. No one, that is, except Hardy, who seems to find these scenes more real than the present. This poem, in contrast to the preceding ones which seek exclusively to recover Emma during her courtship days, illustrates the dangers of a journey into the past – it may overwhelm the present.

COMMENTARY

After the great poems tracking Emma 'through the dead scenes' (line 10 in 'After a Journey') as a means of recovery from the pain of bereavement, this poem seems emotionally to be something of a throwback to earlier poems in the sequence which record Hardy's despair. There is still a return to the past, but this is not entirely memory and the apparent reminiscences seem curiously second-hand – which they are, the details coming from Emma's **memoir**, *Some Recollections*. There is, then, an unconscious **irony**, for Hardy's complaint in the poem is that it is the *present* which feels

CONTEXT

In Emma Hardy's memoir *Some Recollections,* she mentions the tune of the four-hourly chimes of St Andrew's Church 'with its haltings and runnings'. Later she describes riding near Boscastle: 'scampering up and down the hills on my beloved mare alone … The villagers stopped to gaze when I rushed down the hills.'

QUESTION

Judith Fetterley in *The Resisting Reader* (1978) argues that women readers need to be especially alert when reading male-authored texts. They should 'read against the grain', that is refuse to be passive, unresisting readers. How might 'reading against the grain' help to illuminate the strengths and weaknesses of Hardy's portrayal of women?

second-hand to one for whom memories have 'a savour that scenes in being lack' (24). The description of Emma as a child is unremarkable – 'little girl of grace' (4) and the 'sweetest the house saw' (5) – and she is linked, somewhat conventionally, with natural beauty ('like the bud of a flower', 9); perhaps more significantly, she is associated with a vanished way of life, as **symbolised** by the church bells, now silenced, to which she used to listen when lying in bed. These events, we are told, took place in 'the hollow of years ago' (2) – an **image** which suggests not only how they have been almost erased by time but also how determined Hardy is to burrow into the past.

Stanza 3 draws on Hardy's own memories of Emma during the courtship years in Cornwall ('here', 15), since he had seen her riding on Boterel Hill himself (although again the details are from her **memoir**). And this **stanza** certainly evinces more vitality and conviction than the previous two (Emma's 'airy flush outbid / Fresh fruit in bloom', 17–18). However, following the vision of Emma's childhood, this more personally-felt recollection seems to trigger in Hardy a mood of utter desolation: 'to-day is beneaped and stale, / And its urgent clack / But a vapid tale' (26–8). Poetically, this is superior to almost everything that has gone before: Hardy can find nothing of interest in the present, for all its noise and bustle. The image suggested by the 'urgent clack' is that of a train clattering noisily, but purposelessly, over railway tracks. The characteristic sound of the carriages in motion is echoed in the **rhythms** of the final two lines. There is also a criticism here of what Hardy saw as the frenetic meaninglessness of the twentieth century, into which he felt, as an old man, he had strayed. He often used the railway as a symbol of an anti-human progress which was destructive of an older and better way of life – both Emma and the days of their courtship belonged to that former time. However, Hardy's attempts elsewhere to reclaim the past usually have the virtue of providing a basis for a renewal of the present. But here the dangers of tracking through the past are clear: the dead can stifle the living.

HEREDITY

- The poem describes how individuals inherit the 'family face'; it lives on after they die.

GLOSSARY

4 **anon** following

The voice we hear in this poem is that of the 'family face' (1), speaking for the inherited characteristics which are passed from generation to generation even though the individuals that bear them die. It is often difficult to pin down these characteristics which determine resemblance, but they are, **paradoxically**, immortal.

CHECK THE BOOK

'The story of a face which goes through three generations or more, would make a fine novel or poem of the passage of Time' (Hardy's Notebook February 1899 and quoted in his autobiography). Hardy used the idea in *The Well-Beloved* (1892): seeking ideal beauty, Jocelyn Pierston, a sculptor, falls in love with Avice Caro, and then her daughter and her granddaughter. Failing in his artistic quest, and now ageing himself, he settles for marriage with an elderly widow!

COMMENTARY

After reading Darwin, Hardy became interested in the idea of heredity. In this poem, he identifies something 'in man' which is 'eternal' (11), which can defy the processes of time. Inherited characteristics leap across the years and generations while 'Flesh perishes' (2); they 'Despise the human span / Of durance' (9–10) and refuse to die. Hardy **ironically** plays off the 'eternal' nature of inherited characteristics in this poem against the normal human perceptions of time and change. And he points up the further irony that these enduring features are so elusive, surfacing in 'curve and voice and eye' (8), but always amount to a recurring likeness. The voice of the 'family face' we hear is appropriately vigorous, confident, even cocky and mischievous – perhaps something of a malign sprite.

It has been suggested that Hardy really does see these inherited characteristics which survive individual lives as evidence of the eternal in human beings – a kind of Darwinian version of Plato's theory of 'forms', that is to say, the unchanging, timeless forms which underlie, but shape, everything in the everyday, transient world of experience (see also **Critical approaches: Themes** and **Background: Historical background** on Hardy's interest in Darwinism). But this is surely much too optimistic a reading of the poem: rather, Hardy sees heredity as another cruel trick played on the individual in a Darwinian universe, further evidence of our lack of freedom, for we are bound to reproduce the characteristics and traits of our ancestors. It is known that Hardy believed himself to be the last representative of a dying family, cursed by some inherited (but obscure) blood legacy.

THE OXEN

- An old countryman recalls the folk tradition that the oxen kneel at midnight on Christmas Eve.
- A non-believer in a sceptical age, Hardy nevertheless wishes it were true.

This poem records a folk tradition Hardy had heard from his mother. It is midnight on Christmas Eve, and one of the older members of a group of country people gathered around the fireside says that the oxen are kneeling, as they have always done at that time. The listeners picture the scene, although such beliefs are unfashionable now that religious faith is in decline. And Hardy, who is numbered among the sceptics, says that, if asked, he would go to the remote farmyard where the animals are in the hope that it might be true.

CHECK THE POEM

Hardy suggests regret for the decline of faith in other poems, for example in 'The Darkling Thrush'. Elsewhere he expresses a more jaundiced view of Christianity, in a measured way in 'Afternoon Service at Mellstock' but more caustically in 'A Christmas Ghost Story' (where a dead soldier wonders what happened to Christ's message of peace) and 'Christmas: 1924' (with its mention of 'poison-gas', 4).

COMMENTARY

This poem is somehow the more poignant because of its first publication (in *The Times* on 24 December 1915) during the course of a brutal world war. It is informed by nostalgia for a lost faith and lost beliefs – perhaps, too, lost childhood and a vanishing rural community life. Yet all this is suggested by very simple means, which themselves contribute to the poignancy of the poem. The act of faith of the first two **stanzas**, which is also a reclaiming of the past, is gently undermined by the scepticism of the present in the second half of the poem. The change hinges on the description of the belief as a 'fancy few would weave' (9) nowadays, that it is a fiction with no basis in fact. But it is an appealing fiction, and it is significant that Hardy awaits the invitation to test its truth (in a remote farmyard remembered from childhood) while knowing really that no one will ask – thus not quite closing the door of doubt on it.

It is worth examining the **metrical** plot of the poem as it moves from past (in stanzas 1 and 2) to present (in stanzas 3 and 4). Essentially, the poem conforms to the 'common metre' found in **ballads** and hymns: **quatrains**, made up of alternately rhymed **iambic tetrameters** and **trimeters**. But there are variations here, notably the lilting **anapaests** in the first two stanzas, which underpin the nostalgia for the past (e.g. 'An elder said as we sat in a flock', 3), and the more rigorous iambics of the final two stanzas, reinforced by **alliteration** (e.g. 'So fair a fancy few would weave', 9), which denote the shift to a more sceptical present.

THE LAST SIGNAL

- Approaching his friend's funeral, Hardy sees a flash of reflected light on the top of the coffin.
- He believes this to be a gesture of farewell from his friend.

The Dorset **dialect**-poet William Barnes was buried on 11 October 1886. As Hardy approaches the graveyard where Barnes's funeral is under way, the plaque on the coffin catches a ray of the sinking sun; the flash stands out vividly against the sombre cloud in the east. Hardy interprets this as a 'wave' (16) of farewell from his friend and mentor.

COMMENTARY

It would be a mistake to find evidence in this poem of a belief in the workings of the supernatural. Hardy does not suppose for one minute that the dead man has actually communicated with him – the only messages here are Hardy's own. But Hardy's consciousness has been stimulated by the accidental reflection to imagine a moment of human communion in the face of time, death and nature. The process is very similar to that going on in the core Cornwall poems of the 1912–13 sequence. As in those cases, where the communication is in reality only one-way, the dead find ways of breaking their silence.

CONTEXT

William Barnes (1801–86) was buried at Winterborne-Came Church (near Hardy's home, Max Gate) where he had been vicar. They had been friends since 1856. Hardy admired Barnes's use of dialect as well as the wide variety of verse forms and language effects in his poems. Hardy edited the *Select Poems of William Barnes* published in 1908.

CHECK THE POEM
Hardy raises the same issue about poetic fidelity to the dead in 'A Circular'.

CHECK THE POEM
Perhaps the most famous of Anglo-Saxon poems is the epic *Beowulf* (sixth–eighth century AD). The hero Beowulf kills the monster Grendel, who has been attacking the hall of the king and killing his warriors, and later a dragon. A superb new translation of *Beowulf* by the Irish poet Seamus Heaney was published by Faber & Faber in 2000.

GLOSSARY
6 **beating** tramping
22 **on the beat** both 'walking on' and 'performing daily habits'

The 'sudden shine' (10) is not only the gleam from the coffin lid; it is also **symbolic** of Barnes's uniqueness as an individual human being when alive. Might poetry betray the dead by failing to faithfully reproduce their 'shine'? One of the ways Hardy seeks to be faithful to Barnes here is by emulating his use of the **metrical** patterns of ancient Celtic poetry, for example, **rhyming** words at the end of a line with those in the middle of the next (such as 'road' in line 1 with 'abode' in line 2, and 'meant' in line 9 with 'sent' in line 10) and the use of consonantal patterns within individual lines (such as 'That sudden shine sent from the livid east scene', 10). Moreover, Barnes's enthusiasm for the techniques of Anglo-Saxon verse is echoed in the poem's use of **alliteration** ('Something flashed the fire of the sun that was facing it, / Like a brief blaze on that side', 7–8) and exploitation of **compound epithets** ('yew-boughed', 'grave-way', 2, 15) – a feature of Hardy's craft which he had largely acquired from Barnes. But the attempt to capture Barnes's 'shine' (10) is not restricted to his poetic accomplishment: the coffin lid which flashes as it reflects the 'brief blaze' (8) from the sun momentarily calls to mind Barnes's gregarious nature, and specifically 'a farewell … signalled … As with a wave of his hand' (15–16).

THE FIVE STUDENTS

- Five walkers set out on a symbolic life-journey.
- As the seasons pass, they drop out one by one as death claims them – leaving only the poet who knows his time will come too.

On a late spring day, the poet and four companions stride purposefully forth. In high summer one of the company drops out. Autumn comes and still the walkers press on, until another member of the group falls by the wayside. As winter approaches there are only two left. By the end of the year, only the poet remains on the road – but he knows that he too must give up shortly. The journey **motif** provides Hardy with the opportunity to reflect on the course of his life, tracing patterns in his own experience. In particular, he meditates on the deaths of four people who were close to him (though in reality they were never together like this).

COMMENTARY

Despite the title, the course followed here is not an academic one but life itself. The **metaphor** of life as a journey is a common one; here it is linked to the changing seasons (compare this with the passage of time in 'Afterwards'). The consequence is a sense of the remorseless march of time and its toll on the living. The word-portraits of the seasons in each **stanza** are detailed and effective – partly because Hardy was a man who 'used to notice such things' (as he says of himself in 'Afterwards', 4), and partly because, like Darwin (see **Critical approaches: Themes** and **Background: Historical background**), he was impressed by the **paradox** that nature was both a place of struggle and death, and a site of vitality and endless variety.

Perhaps this paradox also accounts for the complex metrical pattern of the poem: only the second and fourth lines of each stanza have the same number of **feet** (they are **iambic trimeters**; the other lines in each stanza are, in order, **iambic tetrameters, pentameters, hexameters** and **dimeters**). This variety allows for much flexibility of **rhythm** in the poem and provides for a tension between positive and negative **cadences** which matches the thematic tension between vitality and death. The early lines in the first four stanzas are vigorous, both in the choice of words and rhythm, suggesting a correspondence between the energies of nature and the determination of the 'students'. The rhythm slows, however, in the **refrain** (reminiscent of **ballad** form) with its **incremental repetition** in line 5, which in every case records loss. The tone is much more sombre and reflective in the final lines of each stanza and arrests the forward drive of the preceding lines.

Time triumphs in the final stanza as death closes in on Hardy. Winter claims the landscape ('Icicles tag the church-aisle leads', 25) and throughout the stanza the heavy, leaden rhythms match the deathly scene. Indeed, the rhythm threatens to collapse entirely in

> **CONTEXT**
>
> Scholars have disagreed on the identity of the five students: 'dark He' was identified by Hardy as Horace Moule (d. 1873) and 'fair She' is almost certainly Emma Hardy (d. 1912); 'dark she' could be either Tryphena Sparks (d. 1890) or Helen Holder (Hardy's sister-in-law, d. 1900); 'fair He' may be either Henry Moule (Horace's brother, d. 1904) or Hooper Tolbart (an old friend of Hardy's, d. 1883). The fifth student is, of course, Hardy himself.

the final line. 'One of us' (Hardy himself) alone remains – and after an emotional pause comes confirmation that all the others are 'gone' (29), the deferral of the word until the end of the line giving it an awful finality. The terse concluding words of the poem, with their grim pun on 'rest' (30) (suggesting both 'remainder', i.e. Hardy, the last of the travellers and soon to die himself, and 'release' from the pain of loss), are actually very eloquent in communicating Hardy's desolation.

THE SHADOW ON THE STONE

CONTEXT

In his autobiography, Hardy says the Druid stone was found buried in the garden by the builders of Max Gate in 1891, 'with a quantity of ashes and half-charred bones' beside it – suggesting a connection with much earlier habitation of the area. Hardy had it re-erected. Emma is said to have burnt his love letters nearby and so Hardy may have associated the stone with the painful latter years of his relationship with her.

- The shadows cast by a nearby tree on a large stone bring to Hardy's mind the outline of Emma when she was gardening nearby.
- He refuses to turn and look and thus dispel the illusion that her ghost is actually there.

Walking by the Druid stone which stands in the garden of Max Gate, his Dorchester home, Hardy thinks that the shadow cast on it by a tree resembles that of Emma when she gardened nearby. It is as if the woman whose loss he had come to terms with is standing behind him, but he refuses to turn and extinguish the hope that her ghost might really be there as the old feelings are stirred in him.

COMMENTARY

This poem, which was first drafted in 1913, should be read in the light of the *Poems of 1912–13* sequence. There, Hardy had, finally, managed to distance himself from his dead wife; here, he refuses to suppress the resurgence of his old affection for her.

Hardy poignantly rewrites the story of Orpheus, who was given permission to bring his dead wife back from the underworld on condition that he did not look back when leading her to the surface. Hardy also alludes to the story at the beginning of 'At Castle Boterel'. Unlike Orpheus, Hardy here resists the temptation to look back. He does so not out of love, but because he fears that she is not there at all. Thus, as he leaves the 'glade' (21) (like Orpheus returning from the underworld), doubt is present but he keeps open the possibility that Emma is indeed there. This is of course only a 'dream' (24) (and the poem suppresses any supernatural explanation for the event) but it is very compelling nevertheless: the poem finally comprises a very human act of faith which challenges the realities of time and death.

Part of the appeal of the poem is its restrained, even tentative, tone as Hardy reflects on the situation. This derives partly from the sustained speech **rhythms**, and the sense that Hardy is confiding in the reader. Doubt and faith are kept in fine tension in this poem, most notably in the double negative 'Nay, I'll not unvision' (19), where, with the use of the 'un'-compound he has coined, Hardy refuses to erase the possibility his heart longs for but which his head tells him is impossible. Hardy's **paradoxical** notion that inanimate rock carries traces of the human activities which have occurred in its vicinity can also be found in 'At Castle Boterel'.

> **CHECK THE POEM**
> In 'The Self-Unseeing', Hardy regrets his failure to look 'behind', that is to appreciate the fullness of the moment; but here there is a reversal of this as he *refuses* to turn and look to see if Emma's ghost is actually there.

IN TIME OF 'THE BREAKING OF NATIONS'

- The endless cycle of agricultural work continues while the political arrangements of Europe change.
- The poet suggests that the story of the lovers will outlast the history of battles.

> **GLOSSARY**
> 1 **harrowing** breaking up, levelling
> 6 **couch-grass** a weed burnt off at the end of the growing season
> 9 **wight** man; Hardy has chosen to use an archaic term (usually meaning 'human being' or 'person')

'The Breaking of Nations' is a reference to the Old Testament: 'Thou art my battle axe and weapons of war: for with thee will I break in pieces the nations, and with thee will I destroy kingdoms' (Jeremiah 51:20). Jeremiah contrasts scenes of political strife and discord with scenes affirming the regenerative cycles of pastoral life.

Writing during the First World War, Hardy is keen to celebrate the unremarkable – but in some ways extraordinary – lives and work of ordinary people in contrast to that version of history which deals with great events. The man and the horse harrowing clods in the ploughed field; couch grass being burnt off: the endless round of work on the land will go on year in, year out, while the hereditary rulers of Europe fall and are lost in history. Above all, the maid and her lover, who repeat the ancient story of romance, are seen to have more significance than the chronicles of war.

COMMENTARY

Hardy said that this poem developed from an idea he had during the Franco-Prussian War (in 1870) but was not written until the First World War was under way. 'Dynasties' (8) is a reference to the Napoleonic Wars (1800–15) which ended at the Battle of Waterloo: Hardy's **epic** drama *The Dynasts*, which deals with this period, was published between 1903 and 1908. Hardy's point is that the figures mentioned in the poem will never appear in a conventional history book yet embody more human value and significance than the battles being fought in France. Dynasties will fall, but the 'maid and her wight' (9), by marrying and having children, will make a greater contribution to the story of the human race.

QUESTION

Compare this poem with 'Drummer Hodge', which also considers the relationship between ordinary lives and the ambitions of powerful rulers.

Hardy was deeply suspicious of versions of history which were preoccupied with the exercise of power to the exclusion of the remarkable stories of ordinary men and women. In fact, many of his poems offer those stories (including his own) as a challenge to the processes of time. Here the 'maid and her wight' assume their roles in the timeless story of romance, in contrast to the strictly relative and specific events recorded in 'War's annals' (11). This privileging of (human) stories is reinforced by the poem's form, particularly the echoes of folk-song in the **rhythms** and the **allusion** to the stories of **ballad** (the 'maid and her wight'). Moreover, the poem's apparent simplicity is deceptive. The numbered **stanzas** seem unconnected and the unity of the poem is perhaps disclosed only after several readings. The use of the phrase 'whispering by' (10) to describe the arrival on the scene of the 'maid and her wight' is very effective: they are so anonymous, so unremarkable, but on reflection, so astonishing – which might also describe the method of the poem itself.

AFTERWARDS

- Hardy writes his own elegy and hopes to be remembered as a countryman.

In this poem Hardy writes his own self-**elegy** – not, it has to be said, as the public figure (the author) but as a countryman who expects to be judged by his neighbours. In a series of stanzas Hardy wonders whether after his death, others will remember him as a man who noticed the beauties of early summer, who was familiar with the flight of the nighthawk at dusk, who tried to protect animals from suffering, who had an eye for the mysteries of the heavens, and who noticed the way the sound of the church bells was carried on the breeze.

COMMENTARY

Here, at the age of 77 (he was in fact to live for another ten years), Hardy writes about his own death as if from beyond the grave. The poem in this sense confirms the **image** he had of himself after Emma's death as 'a dead man held on end' ('The Going', 38). But, just as in the poems about Emma, there is an attempt to bring the 'dead' person to life as Hardy not only talks about the things that mattered to him, but seeks to identify his uniqueness as an individual. The poem achieves this effectively, both through its slow, gentle rhythms which represent Hardy's self-effacing manner, and through the detailed images of nature in each stanza which confirm that he was indeed 'a man who used to notice such things' (4). These merit close attention not just because they are so vivid (Hardy's genius for the **compound epithet** is very evident here: see **Critical approaches: Language and style**) but because embedded in them too is a record of those moments when Hardy imagines himself passing from life to death – for example, the 'eyelid's soundless blink' (5), which both describes the flight of the hawk and represents the moment of death. The poem concludes with Hardy envisaging his own funeral.

CHECK THE POEM

'Afterwards' echoes lines in Thomas Gray's 'Elegy Written in a Country Churchyard' (1751), a poem which meditates upon the lives of the country-folk who now lie buried in the churchyard. The speaker concludes by speculating about what 'some hoary-headed swain may say' about him after his death. The title of *Far from the Madding Crowd* (1874) also derives from Gray's poem.

Indeed, the poem is quietly insistent on the passage of time. This is achieved in part by the repetition of 'when' in each **stanza**, which provides the context for Hardy's 'tremulous stay' (1) on earth and inevitable but unremarkable death (he sees himself as slipping out of the back door of life). The sense of passing time is reinforced by the duration of a day, which is also the passage of the seasons, from a bright morning (in May) through dusk (autumn) and finally to night (winter). This is a convention of **elegy** but there is nothing routine about Hardy's use of it. There is even a suggestion that the process is completed, with Hardy being reabsorbed into the natural world and the return of spring in the last stanza. Notice how the 'outrollings' of the bell 'rise again' (18, 19). There is no sense of a resurrection in religious terms here, but there certainly is a suggestion that Hardy can be 'resurrected' in the memories of those who knew him, and in the poem itself. This is another way in which Hardy attempts to show that human consciousness – here, surviving minds which bear the traces of memory of those who have gone – resists the passage of time. Hardy is so often labelled as a pessimist, but there are grounds for seeing this as a quietly optimistic poem.

AN ANCIENT TO ANCIENTS

- Hardy laments the passing of his intellectual and artistic generation: pleasure and passion lie in the past, the world has changed, death awaits and the young are eager to succeed them.
- However, Hardy asserts that there are many examples of men who have produced great art and added to human knowledge in their old age.

Here Hardy addresses the 'thinning ... ranks' (17) of his ageing contemporaries. For them dancing and music (which from his youngest days held a particular appeal for Hardy), rowing, sailing, flirtations and love itself are all in the past; death is beginning to claim them. Hardy lists the dances and the operas, and the creative artists who were popular when he and his fellows were young men but which have succumbed to new and, for him apparently uncongenial, fashions and tastes. However, Hardy, thinking of himself, is keen to point out that some celebrated writers and thinkers continued to produce work of genius late in life. In particular, he mentions the ancient dramatists and poets, philosophers, historians and scholars whom he read as a young man and whose pessimism and stoicism shaped his own outlook on life. He concludes by addressing the coming generation itself. There is much the Old Guard can bequeath to the young even though some things have eluded them. And there remains much for the young to do as the aged step aside.

COMMENTARY

This is an important poem which touches on Hardy's late flowering as a poet and provides a justification for his second career and prolific output in later years (he wrote all his major poems after the age of 50, and this one was written at the age of 80). His notebooks after 1900 indicate an interest in other elderly artists and writers – some of whom are mentioned in this poem – who continued to be creatively productive. Hardy, already a grand old man of English letters, wished to emulate such men. This was not just a matter of ambition (although Hardy was clearly very pleased with his achievement) but also, as this poem implies in the final lines, a belief that experience and understanding, retrospection and memory provide the means and materials of great **lyric** poetry.

This is a very confident poem and its argument is initially based on accumulating contrasts of youth and age, then and now, optimism and gloom, daybreak and evening. The activities and emotions of 'sprightlier times' (5) are set against images of decay and death, of loss and regret. The variations on the **ballad** form are used effectively. Here the **refrain** ('Gentlemen') is used to arrest the forward movement of the verse and it provides an appropriate sense of regretful, and sometimes **ironic**, reflection on the memories and changes recorded. On occasion the **metrical** regularity is broken, with the aid of a heavy **caesura**, as in lines 4 and 5, when the poet emphasises the decaying present in contrast to better times gone by.

The tone of the poem, however, changes dramatically in stanza 8. Here the 'And yet' (50) signifies a note of resistance after the

> **CONTEXT**
>
> The *Bohemian Girl* (1843) (line 26) is one of the best known operas by Dublin-born Michael Balfe (1808–70); *Il Trovatore* (1853) (line 27) is by Giuseppe Verdi (1813–1901), an Italian composer.

> **CONTEXT**
>
> The novelists are Edward Bulwer-Lytton (1803–73), an historical novelist; Walter Scott (1771–1832), best known for his historical novels such as *Waverley* (1814) and *Ivanhoe* (1819); Alexandre Dumas (1802–70), the French historical novelist; and George Sand (1804–76), the French novelist of rustic life. Alfred Tennyson (1809–92) was considered by many to be the outstanding Victorian poet.

CONTEXT

The painters are William Etty (1787–1849), known for his figure studies; William Mulready (1786–1863), renowned for genre paintings of contemporary life; and Daniel Maclise (1806–70) who favoured historical and literary themes.

CONTEXT

The best known of the classical writers mentioned are Homer (ninth–eighth century BC), author of *The Iliad* and *The Odyssey*, and Sophocles (496–406 BC), writer of **tragic** plays including *Oedipus the King*, *Antigone* and *Electra*. The ideas and teaching methods of Socrates (469–399 BC) appear in the *Dialogues* of his pupil Plato (c. 427–348 BC).

GLOSSARY

14 **inurns** buries

deathly weariness of the previous **stanza** in the face of the 'press' (46) of the upcoming generation. In a reversal of what has gone before, Hardy asserts that there are many examples of ageing writers and artists who have demonstrated the same energy and ambition as the young, and he goes on to list some of them in stanza 9. These individuals, Hardy says, 'Burnt brightlier towards their setting day' (62). This notion is somewhat anticipated by the recognition in preceding stanzas that literary styles and tastes have changed – and Hardy could not have been unaware of the part his poetry had played in this. The decay of the 'bower we shrined to Tennyson' (36) denotes the decline of Tennysonian musicality in poetry – even though Hardy claimed to be an admirer; further, Hardy says that 'throbbing romance has waned and wanned' (32). Hardy's 'harsh' and 'unromantic' poetry had been criticised by many contemporary reviewers (see **Critical approaches**) and his apparent regret for the (literary) past here seems more ambivalent.

The poem ends superbly when the reader realises that the 'Gentlemen' being addressed are no longer Hardy's ageing contemporaries but the coming generation – those who are eager to push aside the Old Guard and make their own mark in the world. Here, Hardy both acknowledges the inevitable and stakes his own claim for recognition. He cautions the young for being impatient to supplant their predecessors – for their time will also come, **ironically**, in a double sense: they will have their achievements, but they too will eventually have to give way to the *next* generation.

SNOW IN THE SUBURBS

- Snowfall transforms a city street scene.
- A sparrow dislodges snow on the branches of a tree; the watchers open the door to let a cat in.

The poem opens with a description of a snowfall in a suburban street and the way the scene is altered. A sparrow is almost buried when, alighting on a branch, it dislodges the snow; this sets off a further cascade. A black cat tentatively and hopefully approaches a house door and the observers let it in. It would be a mistake to read too much into this poem, to seek **symbolic** meanings. Its deeper significance, if any, lies in what it implies about the nature of poetry itself.

COMMENTARY

This is a clever poem which seeks to erase itself in the same way that the snow obliterates the suburban scene. Economic in style from the outset, the poem reduces itself to nothing. The **rhythms** of the poem convey what movement there is in the scene, but this is towards stillness as the falling snow eclipses the stirrings of life in the poem – the sparrow and the cat. The covering effects of the snow are represented in the poem's shape which, with appropriate irregularity emulating the swirling movement of the snow, occupies increasingly less space on the page – finally narrowing down to monosyllabic words, and the closing door. The page – and the street – are left in blank silence.

The poem strives to give the illusion of **impersonality** and it is really only at the end that we become aware of an observer. After all, then, the reader is forced to consider the poem as an artefact, contrived by a human mind. We realise that the poem exists only because of the poet's consciousness, deploying language to organise the randomness of experience, selecting the detail and patterning it in the ways suggested above. It is this awareness of itself as a verbal construct as well as its minimalist style that have led some critics to see this poem as **modernist** – and specifically **imagist** – in its attempt to capture moments in time.

 CHECK THE POEM

The poem makes an interesting contrast with a much later poem entitled 'The Thought-Fox' by Ted Hughes which appeared in a collection entitled *The Hawk in the Rain* (1957). Hughes's poem is about the inspiration which prompts the writing of a poem – in this case a fox.

CONTEXT

Donald Davie (in *Thomas Hardy and British Poetry*, 1972) calls the poem 'an Imagist equation'.

NOBODY COMES

- Night falls and the telegraph wires hum as the wind blows through them.
- A car races past and into the night leaving the poet standing forlornly by the gate.

GLOSSARY

6 **spectral** ghost-like

6 **lyre** an ancient (u-shaped) harp

11 **whangs** makes a loud noise, like a bullet or shot flying through the air (not a word Hardy made up)

CONTEXT

In September 1924, Hardy's second wife, Florence, was operated on in a London hospital for throat cancer. Hardy was 84 and had been married to Florence for ten years. Hardy's anxiety was intense especially as it had been decided that he would not accompany his wife to London (see Millgate, 1985).

CHECK THE BOOK

That 'nobody comes' to relieve lonely depression is a recurrent **motif** in Hardy's work. In *Jude the Obscure* (1895) Jude is described as feeling sorry for himself because learning Latin and Greek entails so much work: But nobody did come, because nobody does' (Ch. 4).

GLOSSARY

6 **leaze** (*dialect*) pasture

This poem opens with a surreal landscape in which nature and the new twentieth-century technologies are uneasily **juxtaposed**. Sounds unheard by previous generations fill the evening air: the ghostly hum of telegraph wires and the noise of a passing car. Waiting by the gate, the ageing poet experiences a moment of **existential** loneliness. This poem has been described as self-pitying – but this is one occasion when biographical information (which the precise date alerts the reader to) invites a quite different interpretation.

COMMENTARY

The poem is effectively structured to narrow down to the predicament of the isolated, anxious and silent figure standing by the gate at the end. The vitality seems to be drained from nature here as night falls: 'Tree-leaves labour up and down' (1) and daylight '[s]uccumbs to the crawl of night' (3). The breeze through the telegraph wires makes eerie and ghost-like noises as the familiar sights of day recede. The presence of car and telegraph wire reminds the reader of Hardy's long life and the extent to which the world had changed during his lifetime. The understated **irony** of the poem is that these new-fangled means of communication have, in Hardy's view, served only to disrupt older patterns of community and fellowship. The car 'whangs along in a world of its own' (11) (a hostile incursion into the scene). The poet says 'It has nothing to do with me' (10) and its disappearance intensifies the blackness and loneliness. The bleak final line of the poem – 'And nobody pulls up there' (14) – encapsulates Hardy's pessimism about the prospects for human happiness in this changing world.

HE NEVER EXPECTED MUCH

- Hardy says he never expected much from life and his experience has borne this out.
- Hardy's pessimism has proven to be more in tune with the way life is than the attitudes of others who had higher expectations.

On his eighty-sixth birthday Hardy reflects that life has turned out much as he expected. Even as a child, Hardy's expectations of life were minimal, and the passing years have confirmed this view. People respond to life in different ways – eagerly, serenely, contemptuously – but Hardy's perception that this is a world of cruelty and chance has enabled him to cope with life's vicissitudes. This poem therefore stands as a justification of his pessimism.

COMMENTARY

Much of the appeal of this poem depends upon its wistful, meditative tone: it is indeed the voice of the old man reflecting on a lifetime. The tone is generated in large measure by the **stanza** pattern and the **refrain** in the second line, and also by the sense of a quiet dialogue going on with another old person, in this case the 'World' (1), the abstraction **personified** as so often in Hardy's poetry. At the end of his life, Hardy seems almost to view the world of time and chance ('neutral-tinted haps and such', 19), with which he has so often struggled, as a friend and mentor.

The poem constitutes a distilling of that self-protective detachment from life which has informed so many of the earlier poems. It could be argued that this poem represents the equanimity of old age. Or perhaps the effect of the 'Well …' which opens the poem, in conjunction with the somewhat listless refrain in the second line of each stanza, is to suggest resignation – or simply weariness.

HE RESOLVES TO SAY NO MORE

- Hardy claims to have had a vision of the future but will keep it to himself so as to spare humanity further anguish.
- Human 'progress' seems to have gone into reverse but Hardy will not divulge what he already knows; his foresight may be exceptional but he determines to remain silent.

Hardy intended this poem to mark the closure of his poetic career, and it was actually published after his death. He suggests that he has

 CHECK THE POEM

In lines 5–8, Hardy recalls his low expectations of life even as a child. 'Childhood Among the Ferns' complements this poem and recalls Hardy's wish not to grow up at all.

GLOSSARY

3 **charnel** deathly (a charnel house is a place where corpses or bones are deposited)

12 **Magians** wise men

CHECK THE BOOK

The Book of Revelation (or 'The Apocalypse of St John') in the New Testament, describes the end of the world and the return of Christ. Chapter 6, Verse 8 reads: 'And I looked, and behold a pale horse: and his name that sat on him was Death, and hell followed with him.'

CHECK THE BOOK

The First World War unsettled Hardy's hopes for the progression of the human race; indeed, time almost seemed to be regressing towards more primitive eras. Hardy's interest in time travel may have been stimulated by H. G. Wells's *The Time Machine* (1895) in which the so-called 'Time Traveller' is able to see the future destiny of the human race.

had an apocalyptic vision of the future, but he resolves to take it with him to the grave. Human beings already have more than enough to cope with. The human race seems to be going backwards rather than progressing but Hardy will not reveal what he has seen. Nor will he speak out simply because his foresight goes beyond the mental limitations of others.

COMMENTARY

Hardy assembles the reasons why he will say no more. The **rhetorical** trick Hardy employs here is to seem to withhold meaning while nevertheless putting forward his ideas, and the whole poem exhibits this double movement of deferral and disclosure. The poem has been seen as **modernist** in its silent eloquence. Following the First World War, which dismayed him so much and dashed his hopes for 'evolutionary meliorism' (see **Critical approaches: Themes**), Hardy recognises that humanity can do without more cause of suffering. But he tantalisingly suggests, with the reference to the 'charnel-eyed / Pale Horse' (3–4) of Death, that there is worse to come. With the benefit of hindsight, this seems to be a prediction of the Second World War.

Hardy's reflections on 'Time' in **stanzas** 3 and 4 evince an impatience with the human race. It is **ironic**, he seems to suggest, that while some wise men predict the possibility of time travel (which could reveal the future he already knows but refuses to say anything about), the majority of the human race seems to be moving backwards in time. Hardy thought that the barbarism of the First World War had demonstrated this. Thus he can say that his vision exceeds the 'blinkered sight of souls in bond' (17), an **image** of the mental imprisonment engendered by conventional ideas. Again, the cause of this is not the forces of the universe, but human beings' refusal to grasp the 'truth' which would make them 'free' (18). As a consequence, Hardy's resolution to say no more actually becomes **sardonically** eloquent: the human race doesn't deserve the poet's 'vision' (16).

EXTENDED COMMENTARIES

TEXT 1 – THE CONVERGENCE OF THE TWAIN

In the first five stanzas, the poet imagines the great ship lying at the bottom of the ocean. He then explains that as the ship was being built, its fate was already being determined: the iceberg that would destroy it was also taking shape in the North Atlantic. The inevitable collision between the two takes place in the final stanza.

Critics have disagreed on the theme of this poem. Some see it as an ironic condemnation of human vanity and specifically of **Victorian** technological overreaching ('the Pride of Life that planned her', 3): at the time the *Titanic* was certainly considered to be the summit of engineering achievement, and its owners boasted that it was 'unsinkable'. Other critics have suggested that Hardy's real target was specifically the extravagance of the *Titanic*'s conception as a kind of floating palace for the rich (see stanzas 3 and 4 especially). It is certainly true that after the disaster the ship's luxuriousness attracted much criticism – as indeed did the fact that more first-class passengers survived than those in steerage (the cheapest accommodation). Alternatively, other critics argue that the poem is not simply about human vanity (whether technological or self-indulgent), as this kind of interpretation does not take sufficient account of the workings of the 'Immanent Will' (18) in the latter half of the poem. (For Hardy, this was the power behind existence: see the discussion of this concept in **Critical approaches: Themes**). Rather, the poem can be seen to be about the iron 'Necessity', as Hardy called it, which governs the universe.

'Vanity' was a favourite word used by Hardy to describe nineteenth-century selfishness and egotism, and the pursuit of wealth and pleasure. Thus he doesn't use the word in its superficial modern sense (personal self-regard) but with solemn biblical associations (for example, the preacher in Ecclesiastes I describes 'all the works that are done under the sun' as 'vanity'). Certainly the opening stanzas of the poem carefully deploy contrasts to point up the ironic end for the *Titanic*, far from the 'vanity' and the 'Pride of Life that planned her' (2, 3). Employing rich, emotive **diction**,

---

GLOSSARY

3 **stilly** quietly

6 **thrid** thread

12 **bleared** dimmed, blurred

30 **august** impressive, imposing

 CHECK THE BOOK

Donald Davie is unequivocal about the intention of the poem: it does not present 'a condemnation of technological presumption', but 'very markedly censures the vanity and luxury which created and inhabited the state rooms of the ocean liner' (*Thomas Hardy and British Poetry*, 1972).

 CHECK THE POEM

Other poems which see modern technology as representing 'human vanity, / And the Pride of life' (2–3) include 'On the Departure Platform', 'The Photograph', 'Midnight on the Great Western' and 'Nobody Comes'.

CONTEXT

The White Star liner *Titanic* sank on 15 April 1912 after it struck an iceberg in the North Atlantic. Much controversy followed the disaster. It was revealed that inadequate provision of lifeboats meant that only 700 people were saved but 1,513 perished (Hardy knew a number of the celebrities on board who died); furthermore, of those lucky enough to have been rescued, the greater number were first-class passengers rather than those in steerage.

Hardy **juxtaposes** the great ship with the lowly marine life at the bottom of the sea where it now rests. Its boilers 'turn to rhythmic tidal lyres' (6). Its mirrors, which were 'meant / To glass the opulent' (7–8) (Hardy almost seems to take a grim delight in this) are now a place where the 'sea-worm crawls – grotesque, slimed, dumb, indifferent' (9). The 'Jewels' (10) in the ship's extravagant décor lie 'lightless, all their sparkles bleared and black and blind' (12). No wonder fishes stare at the 'gilded gear' (14) and ask 'What does this vaingloriousness down here?' (15) (**ironically**, the question that everyone was asking at the time).

The evidence of the opening **stanzas** tends to suggest that Hardy was more critical of the ship's ostentation than its engineering (which he actually seems to have been impressed by). But in any case this is really only half the story of the poem, for from stanza 6 onwards we get its controlling ironic counterpoint: the ship was being constructed at the same time that the 'Immanent Will' (18) was shaping the iceberg (described in appropriately austere language as 'sinister', 'dissociate', 'shadowy silent', 19, 21, 24) which was to sink it. Hardy emphasises that no human could have predicted this catastrophe, issuing as it did from processes so apparently unrelated.

Is it possible to reconcile the varying critical readings of this poem? Did human beings bring this disaster on themselves because of their 'vanity', or was the sinking of the ship the result of the workings of Necessity, or (to set aside Hardy's abstractions for a moment) pure coincidence? It seems that the poem might be raising the question of whether human beings make their own history or whether it is shaped by external forces. Closer examination of the poem shows that it is deeply ambiguous about these issues.

CONTEXT

Hardy wrote this poem for inclusion in a souvenir programme of an opera concert in aid of the *Titanic* disaster appeal.

The poem's ambiguities reside to a considerable extent in the hidden meanings of the words it employs. Again and again Hardy uses words which convey an **antithetical** sense of things being either self-willed (that is, expressing vanity) or shaped by external forces (that is, directed by the Immanent Will, or fate, part of some pre-ordained plan). Thus the *Titanic* is described as 'smart' (22), which means both 'stylish, fashionable' and (an older meaning) 'stinging, painful', referring especially to 'the pain resulting from punishment for some wrongdoing' (in this case, perhaps vanity) by an external agent. Ship and iceberg are described as being 'bent' on collision (28): 'bent' can mean either 'determined, self-willed' or 'directed by an external force'. Ship and iceberg are seen as being on '**paths coincident**' (29): 'coincident' can mean 'occurring together' (brought about by individual actions) or 'in agreement' (indicating an underlying unity or plan). The collision takes place '**anon**' (30) which can mean 'soon' (that is, at some unspecified time of an individual's choice) or (an even older meaning) 'in unity' or 'in one course or direction' (that is, planned for a certain time). The collision is described as an '**august event**' (30): 'august' means 'impressive, imposing' but also brings to mind the word 'augury' (that is, an omen which is subsequently brought to fruition).

> **CONTEXT**
>
> The salamanders (line 5) of legend were reptiles which lived in fire, but Hardy probably, and ironically, means 'inextinguishable' here (the reference is to a red-hot iron used for lighting pipes, gunpowder, etc.)

Ambiguity, then, is the keynote of this poem. It might seem that Hardy is raising (without attempting to resolve) alternative possibilities: either there is an external fate operating in the world which led to the sinking of the *Titanic*, or human vanity was to blame. But there is a third possibility, which is that Hardy thought that humanity was both the prisoner of the web of fate *and* the maker of its own destiny. To put it another way, reckless behaviour in a world of chance and time invariably ends in disaster (as is often the case in Hardy's novels).

Hardy certainly thought for a time that collective human effort and determination might influence the Immanent Will and make the world a better place: this hope formed part of his 'evolutionary meliorism' (see **Critical approaches: Themes**). And is it not possible therefore that he thought the obverse was true – that human blindness could provoke fate by stirring the Immanent Will to malign intervention? The First World War shattered Hardy's hopes for humanity and there is in his last poems (such as 'He Resolves to Say No More') an even bleaker perception of the workings of Necessity as well as a deepening sense of exasperation with the folly of the human race. That the two might be linked is explored in 'The Convergence of the Twain'.

If this is the case it goes some way to explaining a further ambiguity in the poem. There is an extended **metaphor** of marriage working

CHECK THE BOOK

Donald Davie, who can be critical of Hardy's versification, writes (in *Thomas Hardy and British Poetry*, 1972): 'The poem itself is an engine, a sleek and powerful machine; its rhymes slide home like pistons inside cylinders.'

QUESTION

Claire Tomalin (in *Thomas Hardy*, 2007) describes the poem as 'grim and exuberant at the same time'. How are these opposite emotions expressed in the poem?

GLOSSARY

8 **chaise** lightweight open carriage

13 **balked of** denied

through the last five **stanzas**. At first this seems odd. In stanza 7 the iceberg is described as a 'sinister mate' (19) for the *Titanic*. Stanza 9 predicts their 'intimate welding' (27). In stanza 10 iceberg and ship are described as 'twin halves of one august event' (30) which achieve 'consummation' (33) (which can mean both 'completion' and 'sexual union in marriage') in stanza 11. If there is a link between the Immanent Will and human actions, then the title of the poem signifies not just the collision of iceberg and ship, but the catastrophic union of vanity and fate.

Finally, the ambiguities of the poem extend to its **metrical** features. The **rhythmic** precision of the poem (evident when read out loud) is meant to emulate the superb engineering of the ship (the vanity which built her), but in its forward drive it catches that inexorable process which leads to the fated collision with the iceberg (the forces of the universe which destroyed her). Each stanza comprises two **trimeters** and one **hexameter**. For the most part strongly **iambic**, these lines echo the rhythm of the ship's pistons, but the occasional, carefully placed **anapaest** and the release into the long third line also suggest the movement of the ship through the water. The forward movement of the verse is dramatically arrested, however, by the heavy stress on 'Now!' (32) and the following **caesura**, effectively mimicking the impact of ship and iceberg. This is the moment that the poem has been building up to. The shock is felt in the verse itself – partly because of the change of tense and the pauses which follow the phrases introduced by the repeated conjunction 'And' (32–3); partly because of the **alliterative** 'c' which evokes a juddering effect in 'consummation comes' (33); and partly because of the use of the word 'jars' (33) itself, which awkwardly echoes the preceding rhymes ('Years'/'hears', 31, 32). It has also been pointed out that the shape of each stanza resembles a ship lying low in the water.

TEXT 2 – AT CASTLE BOTEREL

Hardy seems to be on the point of leaving Cornwall and the scenes of his courtship of Emma. He glances back at the hillside and in his mind's eye he sees himself and Emma as they were forty-three years before: was there ever, he asks, a 'time of such quality … In that hill's story?' (17–18). Emma is now dead but in Hardy's memory her 'phantom figure' (28) remains on that hillside. However, as his own death approaches, he bids farewell to her ghost and the landscape of romance. This is arguably the greatest poem not only of the 1912–13 sequence but of all Hardy wrote. It comprises a powerful effort in consciousness to defeat the processes of time by reclaiming the past, but even here there is an undercurrent of loss and guilt.

'After a Journey', 'Beeny Cliff' and 'At Castle Boterel' form the core of the *Poems of 1912–13*, the sequence of **elegies** Hardy wrote following the death of his wife Emma. After the earlier poems expressing shock and grief, they represent that stage in the elegiac **cycle** when the bereaved person seeks recovery by imagining an ideal **image** of the loved one to compensate for the painful fact of death. 'At Castle Boterel' is Hardy's most convincing attempt to reclaim the past by envisioning the youthful Emma in the landscape of their idyllic courtship (he had undertaken a pilgrimage to Cornwall in 'search' of her). Some commentators have suggested that in this poem love does indeed conquer time, but it may in fact be better to read it as a poem of both reclamation and loss.

The opening stanza alludes to another quester in pursuit of a wife who had died, the Greek mythical character Orpheus. 'I look behind' (3) says Hardy – and it looks as though Hardy's quest is going to fail as did that of Orpheus: he is about to leave the scenes of his courtship, never to return. But just at the moment of departure he pauses to look back and is rewarded by a vision of himself and Emma on the hillside.

Hardy's initial sense of failure is suggested by the drizzle which 'bedrenches the waggonette' (2). But in fact the mist becomes an aid to vision by clouding the reality of the scene behind him ('the fading byway', 3) and enabling a shift into memory and the past (which is what his 'look behind' has now become). Thus he envisions 'Distinctly' (5) – and the memory of 'Myself and a girlish form' (6) is given substance by the recollected physicality of their ascent of the hill all those years ago: the pony was 'sturdy' (9) but the lovers had to alight and make the effort of the climb themselves.

> **CONTEXT**
>
> 'Kastell Boterel' is Cornish for Boscastle. Boterel is a Cornish surname (and probably originates from 'Tibida Boterel' in south-east Brittany). The Boterels settled in Cornwall in the thirteenth century at what is now Boscastle. There are still Boterels living in north-west Cornwall.

> **CONTEXT**
>
> Orpheus is the legendary Greek poet, who set out on a quest to recover his wife, who had died from a snakebite, from the underworld. In Orpheus's case the backward glance as he is about to leave Hades proves disastrous: he loses Eurydice forever. The myth is also referenced in 'The Shadow on the Stone'.

CONTEXT

Hardy might also have been interested in the powers of Orpheus as a poet and singer: it was said he could charm not only men and beasts, but trees and rocks also. It was the music of his lyre that persuaded the gods to agree to his request.

This is a sign, after the hesitant opening of the poem, that Hardy's confidence is growing. The challenge he has set himself here is to convince the reader that the subjective memory (the presence of the two lovers on the hillside and what they stood for) can transcend the objective facts of time and space. The process begins in earnest with a **paradox**: what they did on the hillside is of little consequence – but he says there never was a 'time of such quality … In that hill's story' (17–18). Indeed, though many other walkers have made the ascent ('it has been climbed, foot-swift, foot-sore, / By thousands more', 19–20) their story is unique.

This paradox forms the basis of what is to follow, and much of the power of the poem rests in Hardy's struggle with the contradictions of mind and matter: the landscape is mindless but endures, while human beings have consciousness (the power to love and remember, for example) but are ephemeral. And Hardy does not flinch from recognising that the forces of the universe are ranged against them. There is a keen sense in this poem (as elsewhere) of the intractibility of the material world:

> Primaeval rocks form the road's steep border,
>   And much have they faced there, first and last,
> Of the transitory in Earth's long order (21–3)

The landscape endures while the human beings ('the transitory in Earth's long order') are here today and gone tomorrow. But consciousness, subjective perception – the capacity of the mind to reclaim the past, and invest the landscape with meaning – can challenge those objective facts.

Hardy clinches his point with an astonishing assertion. With an **ironic allusion** to the fossil record which formed part of the supporting evidence for Charles Darwin's argument, he says the rocks themselves still bear traces of the fact that he and Emma were there: 'what they record in colour and cast / Is – that we two passed' (24–5). This is delivered with such conviction, coming where it does in the poem's structure, that we are inclined to believe him. The lovers who were once on that hillside, and Hardy by recalling them, have challenged the passage of time and transformed the enduring landscape.

This enables Hardy to move to the poem's crowning expression of faith. While again acknowledging the objective fact – 'Time's unflinching rigour, / In mindless rote, has ruled from sight / The substance now' (26–8) – his subjective perception is that Emma's 'phantom figure' (28) still remains on the slope. Of course, by any objective standard this is not true; but the illusion is sustained here (although the use of the word 'phantom' quietly reminds the reader, even at this triumphant moment, that it *is* an illusion). Time and space can be measured (and the poem insists on this again and again, for example, 'but a minute', 'ever' (16), 'first and last' (22), and so on), but there is a human, subjective truth – Hardy calls it 'quality' – which transcends mindless matter.

But can love really be said to conquer time in this poem? If so, the reader feels its victory is only momentary. Indeed, this impression is reinforced by the structure of the poem, which moves from the hesitant opening (present), through the growing confidence of the middle section and the vision of the young, beautiful Emma (past), to the faltering, sad conclusion (present). At the end of the poem Hardy reminds us that he is old (his 'sand is sinking', 33) and he takes a final look back at the 'phantom' which is 'shrinking, shrinking' (31) – away from the rain of present reality and the fading light into the past and the grave; and perhaps too, somewhat reproachfully, away from Hardy's attempts at reconciliation on the basis of reawakened love. The co-existence of past and present in the poem has the effect of emphasising the real sense of loss which returns at the end. For the truth is that Time has been doubly destructive in this story: first it killed the love between the couple (the estrangement in their marriage) and then it killed Emma. This gives force to Hardy's final remark: 'I shall traverse old love's domain / Never again' (34–5).

The recovery from grief which concludes the **elegiac cycle** and which here depends upon the envisioning of Emma is achieved only after a struggle in consciousness. This is the final impression which the poem leaves, despite its confident middle section. Ground is won, then lost. This is echoed in the **rhythms** of the poem, which betray a tension between conviction and doubt, recovery and loss. Each **stanza** moves from constraint and hesitation (suggested in the

CHECK THE BOOK

Donald Davie is emphatic that 'love triumphs over time' in this poem, and that Emma is thereby enshrined forever in 'the landscape of memory' (*Thomas Hardy and British Poetry*, 1972).

CHECK THE BOOK

In an essay entitled 'Hardy's Poems of 1913' (in *Thomas Hardy and Contemporary Literary Studies*, ed. by Tim Dolin and Peter Widdowson, 2004), Linda Shires notes that '"old love's domain" carries a triple meaning: the region of a long-term relationship; the landscape of love; and the territory of love as viewed from old age'.

mid-line pauses or **caesurae**, and the alternating **masculine** and **feminine endings** in the first four lines of each **stanza**) to release in the short final line, where conviction and faith prevail. Until, that is, the final short line of the seventh stanza, which seems to shut the door on love and vision with equal certainty.

TEXT 3 – DURING WIND AND RAIN

The scenes of family life described in the poem derive from Thomas Hardy's memories and Emma Hardy's **memoir**, *Some Recollections*. In the first three stanzas there are affirmative accounts of family fellowship (the singing), work (clearing the path, building a seat) and leisure (breakfast on the lawn). The family members lead their lives with an easy assurance and a sense that they will go on forever. They move house (in stanza 4) but take this confidently in their stride. Nevertheless, this scene does denote a change in their lives and provides a link with the recurrent **symbolism** of wind and rain (that is, the destructiveness of time) with which the family activities are counterpointed throughout the poem. Each stanza ends with **images** of destruction as the 'years' take their toll, and finally the rain is described running down the inscriptions on their tombstones. It is a deeply ambivalent poem which may, or may not, contrive to extract some human consolation from a world of change and decay. Hardy considered 'During Wind and Rain' to be among his best and many critics have endorsed this view. The poem has prompted some very different readings. It certainly shows a poignant awareness of the effects of time and change. But how successful is it in resisting those processes?

This poem is retrospective – the past is seen from the perspective of the present. Nevertheless, the whole poem is conducted in the present tense, which suggests a co-existence in the poet's mind of then and now, and reinforces the sense of the passage of time. This tends also to unsettle any simple conclusion that the past is better than the present (which might otherwise seem obvious here). The poem seems to offer a backward glance over a whole life from the vantage point of old age, with the impulse to trace out meaningful patterns. But even by Hardy's standards the narrative restraint in this poem is striking: we are never told who 'they' are. This may be

CONTEXT

Claire Tomalin (in *Thomas Hardy*, 2007) describes this poem as 'a surreal and lyrical **lament** for the Giffords [Emma's family], calling up scenes at their Plymouth home described by Emma: how they had to leave it, and how the years brought everything bright to an end for them'. In other words, while we should be wary of interpreting poems on the basis of biographical details, 'During Wind and Rain' is founded in actual events and people. Indeed, it is also likely that the dominant **refrain** was derived from the phrase used by Emma herself: 'all has been changed with the oncoming years'.

a self-protective manoeuvre, but it certainly has the effect of universalising the experience.

The poem offers a series of images of ordinary human beings engaged in the everyday activities of family life – singing, tidying the garden and building a 'shady seat' (12), having breakfast on the lawn, moving house. But all this is set in the context of the 'years' and at the end of the poem we realise that 'they' are all dead. There seem to be two versions of time active in the poem: ordinary, everyday time within which the business of family life is conducted, and 'Time' – inhuman, cosmic, a fundamental principle of the material universe – which provides the more alien framework within which these activities and lives take place. This is the source of much of the poem's ambivalence.

Each stanza has the same **antithetical** pattern, setting the positive, social, daily activities of the human family against the destructive processes of Time. In part the contrasts are located in the verbs employed as well as the concepts. The family 'sing' (1) (an image of harmony and fellowship); they 'clear' and 'build' (8, 12) (an image of shared work); they are seen 'breakfasting' (15) on the lawn (as if such days will last forever); they 'change' (22) house (a normal part of a family history). But the **ballad**-like refrain on the sixth line of each stanza abruptly reminds us of the passing years, and introduces the changes they have wrought: the 'sick leaves reel down in throngs' (7), the 'white storm-birds wing across' (14), the 'rotten rose is ript from the wall' (21), and finally 'the rain-drop ploughs' (28) down the names carved on the tombstones. In each case the single destructive verb of the last line is **juxtaposed** with the earlier creative verbs. The impact of the last line, and of the refrain which precedes it, is enhanced by a change in the **rhythm**. After the easy-going movement of the first five lines (which confers an informed, lively tone), the refrain is slow and sombre, and it sets up the long final line with its four heavy **stresses**. The **alliteration** and **assonance** which reinforce the (creative) rhythmic qualities of the opening lines of each stanza ('They sing their dearest songs', 1, 'They clear the creeping moss', 8) have a quite different effect in the final lines, where they emphasise the destructiveness of Time ('See, the white storm-birds wing across!', 'And the rotten rose is ript

CHECK THE POEM

The 'sick leaves' in line 7 recall the 'Pestilent-stricken multitudes' in Shelley's 'Ode to the West Wind' (1819). However, it is clear that the wind in this poem is a literal force which shows the action of time; unlike its role in Shelley's poem where it is an imaginative force (which inspires poetic singing). Again, this is a measure of the difference between Hardy and his **Romantic** predecessors.

from the wall', 14, 21). And the contrast between past and present, between order and chaos, between the familiar and the alien, is highlighted by the return to the opening **rhyme** at the end of each **stanza**.

However, the first five lines of each stanza are not entirely immune from the changes which the last two lines confirm: all the activities described take place in a domestic time, but a careful reading might well reveal a sense of fundamental 'Time' in some of the details mentioned. Thus an evening of family singing is recalled: 'Treble and tenor and bass, / And one to play' (3–4). But the reference to 'candles mooning each face' (5) brings to mind the traditional **image** of a burning candle representing the transience of life. We hear about work in the garden (clearing the paths and building a seat), but the reference to the 'creeping moss' (8) reminds us of the way nature can reclaim the sites of human endeavour (and spread over old graves?). They breakfast on the lawn in summer, but the word 'blithely' (15) perhaps suggests a complacency about the effects of Time. 'They change to a high new house' (22) – but it is significant that Hardy chooses the verb 'change' and not 'move'. Finally, the description of the furniture on the lawn prompts thought of other occasions when this might be so – following a death, for instance.

Perhaps Hardy is simply saying that, in a characteristically human way, the family carry on with their lives, for the most part regardless of the fact that they live in a universe of Time and change. The last lines of each stanza undermine this complacency, but the contradictions are managed without **irony** here – or at least the irony is muted. The truth is that they all have died; but their lives, their energy and hopes, their purpose and fellowship ('brightest things that are theirs', 26) which are solidly present in each stanza are not negated by this fact. And this is as true for humans now as it ever was. Hardy's journey into memory, his reclaiming of the past, is a way of reclaiming the present, reminding us of what matters, and resisting the **alienating** effects of Time.

Not every reader would agree with this interpretation. Some critics point to the title and say that the wind and rain stand as the controlling **symbols** in a poem of change and decay, suffering and

CHECK THE BOOK

In the essay 'Hardy as a Nineteenth-century Poet' (in *The Cambridge Companion to Thomas Hardy*, ed. Dale Kramer, 1999), Dennis Taylor says that in 'During Wind and Rain' Hardy emphasises human work as recalling 'what once was but has now passed'. And this, says Taylor, also applies to writing itself, not just on the gravestone but in the form of poetry.

loss. This symbolism is emphasised in the last line of each stanza. The wind makes the 'sick leaves reel down in throngs' (7) – the falling leaves of autumn are a traditional image for Time and mortality. The 'white storm-birds' (14) are harbingers of death hovering over the tidied garden. The 'rotten rose is ript' (21), by the malevolence of Time, from the wall near where the family were 'blithely breakfasting' (15). And all this leads to the final image of the gravestones. Moreover, some critics say the poem also asserts that the past was better than the present, for that is where all the music was to be found.

One way of resolving these different readings is to look carefully at the last stanza. On the face of it the live songs of the opening stanza have been reduced to the dead inscriptions on the tombstones, and there is no doubt that this is one of the meanings of the poem. The preceding stanzas might have conveyed a sense that the individuals mentioned would go on forever, but the truth is that even those busy lives were short and ended in the grave: 'Down their carved names the rain-drop ploughs' (28). The use of the word 'plough' is surprising here. At first it seems that nature (Time) is slowly erasing the record of those names, having already erased the lives themselves. But 'plough' is also an image of cultivation and fertility (compare a similar idea in the poem 'In Time of "The Breaking of Nations"'). And here it is linked with language, the 'carved names'. In this way the tombstones become an ambivalent image, not only of death, but of the antidote to Time and change – the resilience of the human community, of work, language, the importance of memory and poetry itself. Thus an image of destruction is transformed into an image of renewal and in so doing validates the theme and form of the poem itself.

CHECK THE POEM

Dennis Taylor sees Seamus Heaney's wonderful poem 'Digging' (1966) as asserting the same idea about poetry and recollection when Heaney attempts to justify his chosen career as poet as opposed to the skilled labour of his father and grandfather: 'Between my finger and my thumb / The squat pen rests / I'll dig with it'.

PART THREE

CRITICAL APPROACHES

THEMES

PESSIMISM

It was Hardy's apparent preoccupation with the passing of time, the loss of loved ones, failed hopes, and the decline of religious faith that led contemporary reviewers of his poetry to complain about his pessimism (see **Critical perspectives: Original reception**). Certainly the passage of time is a central theme in Hardy's poetry: he seems to have believed that it was the source of all the unhappiness in the world. A related theme concerns his perception of the indifference of the enduring landscape to the short lives of human beings. Hardy thought that humanity was dwarfed by the forces of the universe and, like many others in the latter years of the nineteenth century, he felt a deep sense of **alienation** and personal insignificance. But this is not all we find in Hardy's work, and it is vital to understand that the pessimism evident in dark poems like 'Wessex Heights', which includes **ironic** reflection on his youthful hopes and his mental crisis in 1896, is offset by resistance. In many of his most memorable poems (for example, 'At Castle Boterel', 'During Wind and Rain' and 'Afterwards') the same consciousness that feels pain also struggles against the meaninglessness of space and time, and seeks to reassert the essentially human against the forces of the universe. Acts of memory – attempts to reclaim the past – strive to resist the processes of change and loss in these poems. Related to this, Hardy's visionary insight seeks to imbue the indifferent landscape with human meaning. More generally, the charge that Hardy can only see the **tragic** in human affairs does not take sufficient account of the wry humour, the creative vitality and the commemoration of the simple things of life that permeate his novels and poetry.

Of an innately melancholic disposition, and prone to bouts of black depression, Hardy's outlook on life was shaped by the emerging crisis of confidence in the **Victorian** world in the 1860s and 1870s. Part of the problem was middle-class society itself and its obsession with 'Progress'. It seemed to Hardy that such an **ideology** only intensified individuals' vulnerability to the destructiveness of time because it denied older beliefs, values and customs that conferred a measure of communal security. He could not accept the Victorian notion of divine Providence, a God-given plan for the world, which worked towards good. But for many of his contemporaries in the middle years of the century, the march of time and the development of Victorian middle-class civilisation seemed to be running reassuringly in parallel. Hardy didn't share this optimism (see **Background: Historical background** for further discussion). For him, there was a depressing inevitability about the way middle-class society was making inroads into all areas of life, and it seemed to bring with it a growing sense of loneliness and emptiness. Hardy often used the phenomenon of the railway (reaching into Dorset when he was a young man and dislocating long-established communities and customs) as a **symbol** for this process – running like time itself, inexorably onwards and crushing everything human in its path.

The complacency of the Victorian middle classes was shattered by the publication of Charles Darwin's *On the Origin of Species by Means of Natural Selection: or, The Preservation of Favoured Races in the Struggle for Life* in 1859. Ideas about evolution had been around for many years. The difference in Darwin's case was that he developed a powerful theory to explain it: in the competitive struggle for existence, chance mutations could confer particular advantages on some creatures, which might then develop into new species. The randomness of the process of natural selection made it difficult to believe that history had a design and purpose. Middle-class ideology and Darwinism were allied in Hardy's view: one had drained reality of meaning by putting the doctrine of 'Progress' before human relationships; the other had generated a view of the environment which had reduced human beings to insignificant victims.

Nevertheless, until the mid-1870s, Hardy seems to have remained relatively optimistic about the future. In 1867, his poem '1967' could still envisage a better world by that year – 'A scope above this blinkered time' (9). But it would appear that his view of life became

CONTEXT

Charles Darwin delayed publishing his ideas – fearing the religious controversy that would follow. He recognised that his theory removed humankind from its hitherto central place in the natural order and challenged the ancient narratives of Genesis. When he discovered that Alfred Russel Wallace had reached similar conclusions to his own he rushed to finish *The Origin of Species*. Hardy claimed to be an early admirer of the work, and subsequently attended Darwin's funeral.

PESSIMISM continued

CHECK THE BOOK

The ancient Greek philosopher Aristotle based his definition of tragedy in his *Poetics* on a study of the plays of Aeschylus, Euripides and Sophocles. Tragedy, Aristotle said, achieves a 'catharsis' (usually translated as 'purification') of the audience's emotions through the description of events arousing pity and terror. The tragic hero, a man of high estate, commits a fatal error which leads to his downfall. In particular, Aristotle observed that the hero often displays outstanding human qualities which are seen to be wasted in the tragic outcome. These elements are found in, for example, *Oedipus the King* by Sophocles, which is one of the most famous ancient Greek tragedies.

more melancholic after 1874, the year of publication of *Far From the Madding Crowd*. The novels published after this date – including *The Return of the Native* (1878), *The Mayor of Casterbridge* (1886), *The Woodlanders* (1887) and *Tess of the d'Urbervilles* (1891) – deal, as had their predecessors, with the changes taking place in the countryside but are uncompromisingly **tragic**. Debate on their redemptive aspects (modelled as they are on the Ancient Greek tragedies) has centred on the degree to which the protagonists demonstrate life-enhancing qualities. In the earlier novels *Under the Greenwood Tree* (1872) and *Far From the Madding Crowd* the village rustics have a prominent role and lighten the mood with their gossip and humour (some of these country folk 'lie in Mellstock churchyard', 3, in the poem 'Friends Beyond'); later their influence is diminished and they have disappeared altogether from *Jude the Obscure* (1895) which has predominantly urban settings and which critics generally agree is the one unequivocally pessimistic work.

Jude the Obscure was the last novel; after that Hardy wrote only poetry. Over the coming years, the recurring critical assessment that his poems were pessimistic prompted him, in a prefatory 'Apology' to the volume *Late Lyrics and Earlier* (1922), to deny that he was a pessimist and assert that his poems did not articulate a philosophy of life but were actually 'a series of fugitive impressions which I have never tried to co-ordinate'. He said he preferred to be seen as an 'evolutionary meliorist', that is, someone who believed that the world could be improved by collective human effort. His wish was that 'pain to all upon [the earth], tongued or dumb, shall be kept down to a minimum by loving-kindness' and he stated that an altruistic motive informed all his writing. The effects of loving-kindness are shown in the poem 'At the Railway Station, Upway' where the three characters – boy, convict and constable – achieve a moment of human fellowship prompted by the boy's violin playing.

Hardy's evolutionary meliorism was shaped by his reading of Auguste Comte and John Stuart Mill and reflects his dismay at the decline of faith following the publication of Darwin's *The Origin of Species*. When Hardy's Christian belief dissolved around 1865 he, like many **Victorians**, felt an acute sense of loss and sought to find a substitute for Christianity. While Hardy rejected the notion of a divine Providence, the impulse to believe in some force that shaped experience still remained active and this is the hope expressed in 'Nature's Questioning'. The alternative is randomness, where things simply happen in a meaningless universe, or 'Hap', a favourite word of Hardy's, in the poem of the same name, where he further defines this randomness as 'Crass Casualty' (11). Hardy emphasised that the force he envisaged was indifferent and unconscious and he called it various names including the 'Immanent Will' (in, for example, 'The Convergence of the Twain', 18). By this he meant the abstract principle (it needs to be remembered that he understood this **metaphorically**), which underwrites all personal and public events, the web of fate which circumscribes all human life.

Hardy's disclaimer in the 'Apology' of 1922 did not stem the criticism that his poems were bleak. Again he protested: in an 'Introductory Note' to the volume entitled *Winter Words in Various Moods and Metres* (1928) Hardy said 'My last volume of poetry [*Human Shows, Far Phantasies, Songs and Trifles*, 1925] was pronounced wholly gloomy and pessimistic by reviewers … My sense of the oddity of this verdict may be imagined when, in selecting them, I had been, as I thought, rather too liberal in admitting flippant, not to say farcical, pieces into the collection'. And it is true that his **oeuvre** is punctuated with comic or **satiric** poems. In 'The Ruined Maid', for example, Hardy raises serious issues in a light-hearted manner. He can also be jocular about death as in 'The Levelled Churchyard' where the disturbed corpses complain that they have been 'mixed to human jam' (6). There are the **sardonic ironies** of 'An Ancient to Ancients' where Hardy deflates the pretensions of the coming generation of poets, and the satirical **vignettes** 'In Church', 'In the Restaurant' and 'At the Draper's'. In 'The Children and Sir Nameless' the funereal effigy of the arrogant knight, who loathed the children playing in his park, is placed by the church modernisers under the pews where the children sit, and their restless feet then wear out his name and nose: 'Who was this old stone man beneath our toes?' (24) they ask. In 'The Curate's Kindness, A Workhouse Irony' the well-meaning cleric arranges, contrary to the rules, for husband and wife to remain together in the workhouse – but the husband curses his luck

> **CONTEXT**
>
> John Stuart Mill's *On Liberty* (1859), an essay defending individual freedom, had a considerable influence on Hardy – especially its attack on contemporary Christian practice as being at variance with the precepts of the New Testament. Auguste Comte's *A General View of Positivism* (1848) advocated a 'religion of humanity' as an alternative to Christianity and urged service, compromise and 'loving-kindness'.

because the one compensation in his view for falling on hard times was to free himself of his wife of forty years! He goes off at the end of the poem to commit suicide.

Perhaps contrary to the common view, there are also many positives in Hardy's poetry. He celebrates the simple pleasures of life in 'Great Things' and 'Any Little Old Song'. He talks affectionately in 'Old Furniture' of the traces of past generations in the possessions that gave meaning to their lives. He bears witness to the continuity of human life in 'In Time of "The Breaking of Nations"', and offers love, fellowship and pleasure as the antidote to time and change in 'During Wind and Rain'. More often the poet of romantic heartache, Hardy describes fulfilled love in 'A Church Romance', and is whimsical about unrequited love in 'To Lizbie Brown'. In 'The Last Signal' he manages to extract a positive moment of human connection from the death of his friend.

Hardy hoped that 'loving-kindness' might influence the workings of the Immanent Will for the better. However, the First World War shattered these hopes. By the end of his life Hardy's view that the Immanent Will was utterly indifferent to human life had hardened and he even wondered if it could be tipped into malignity by human folly (see the discussion of 'The Convergence of the Twain' in **Extended commentaries: Text 1**). Towards the end of his life he wrote some deeply pessimistic poems – not least 'A Wish for Unconsciousness' where he longs for oblivion, and 'A Necessitarian's Epitaph' where life is seen as an ordeal he would rather not have experienced.

THE PAST

Why is Hardy so keen to recover the past in poem after poem? It is not because, as has sometimes been claimed, he was incapable of living in the present – although he did recognise that people, himself included, found it increasingly difficult, in the words of the Roman poet Horace, to 'seize the day' (*carpe diem*), that is, make the best use of time before it is too late. This failure is one consequence of the **alienated** consciousness. Nor is Hardy's habit of retrospection simply due to an assumption that the past must be better – although in many poems the past is **ironically** counterpointed with an unhappy present. Hardy was under no illusions: memory might validate the past, but the past *is* past. There is no preventing the passage of time.

In part the answer lies in Hardy's conception of himself as a poet. In his autobiography (and poetically in 'An Ancient to Ancients') Hardy compares himself with other artists who produced their best work late in life noting 'that Homer sang as a blind old man, that Aeschylus wrote his best up to his death at nearly seventy, that the best of Sophocles appeared between his fifty-fifth and ninetieth years, that Euripides wrote up to seventy'. He specifically suggests that only an old poet can write great poetry: 'Among those who accomplished late, the poet spark must always have been latent; but its outspringing may have been frozen and delayed for half a lifetime.' And now the subject-matter for the poems was surfacing into his consciousness: 'I have a faculty ... for burying an emotion in my heart or brain for forty years, and exhuming it at the end of that time as fresh as when interred.' Thus memory, and specifically his own memories, provide many of the subjects for his poetry, Hardy having accepted that the proper subject of his **lyric** poetry was his own subjective life.

This belief in poetry-as-memory accounts for Hardy's characteristic stance of lonely retrospection. The voice we hear is again and again that of an old man, whose life is to all intents and purposes over, looking back on his past. In 'The Going' he describes himself as a 'dead man held on end' (38) – a man who has lived beyond his time, surviving both friends and family. However, this does not preclude (and in some cases it even prompts) visions that defy the materiality of time and space. Hardy's poems often contain visions of a history which privileges human relationships or landscapes imbued with human meanings. And, as one might expect from a writer who persistently plunders memory and the past for his subjects, the poems are haunted by the ghosts of the dead.

It has been noticed that Hardy has a fondness for poems set in graveyards and that there are over sixty such poems in his collected works. These include 'Friends Beyond' where the dead whisper to him, the black humour of 'The Levelled Churchyard', and both

 CHECK THE BOOK
Tim Armstrong makes the point that from the perspective of the outside world Hardy was, when he turned exclusively to the writing of poetry after 1895, 'already a part of posterity, invisible behind the trees surrounding his house, Max Gate, his autobiography written, his portraits painted, and his manuscripts donated to national collections' (Introduction to *Thomas Hardy: Selected Poems*, 1993).

CHECK THE BOOK

In *The French Lieutenant's Woman* (1969), a novel set in the 1860s and a guidebook to the period as well as a mystery story, John Fowles suggests that the urge to elegise, 'to go backwards into the future, mesmerized eyes on one's dead fathers instead of on one's unborn sons', was the most damaging aspect of the **Victorian** age. The hero Charles Smithson learns to free himself from the 'ghostly presence of the past' and look to the future. By this yardstick, Hardy is very much a Victorian.

'Transformations' and 'Voices from Things Growing in a Country Churchyard' where the dead re-emerge, in ways which echo their former vitality, in the flora of the churchyard. Indeed, the notion of a poetic resurrection of the dead is fundamental to Hardy's purpose. In 'Friends Beyond', for instance, the poet recalls the energetic lives of the dead even though they seem content with the oblivion of death. In a further **irony**, though they have forgotten Hardy, he hasn't forgotten them and they will live on forever in his poem. Indeed, Hardy almost seems compelled to resurrect in words the dead whose memories he carries in his brain.

As a consequence Hardy is perhaps pre-eminently the writer of **elegies**. There are elegies for family and friends, lovers, the war dead and pets. Sometimes the dead are recalled, sometimes they speak but often the pattern of the poem includes three common elements: memories of the dead, the passing of time, and the realisation of loss. Emma is resurrected in 'Under the Waterfall' and 'My Spirit Will Not Haunt the Mound' as well as in the best known of Hardy's elegies, the *Poems of 1912–13*. Family members are recalled in 'The Self-Unseeing' (father and mother), 'A Church Romance' (which recalls his parents' courtship), 'The Roman Road' (mother), 'After the Last Breath' (mother), 'One We Knew' (paternal grandmother), 'Logs on the Hearth' (sister Mary) and 'During Wind and Rain' (Emma's relatives). A former lover is eulogised in 'Thoughts of Phena', 'In a Eweleaze Near Weatherbury' and 'The Photograph'; objects of unrequited love are recalled in 'To Lizbie Brown' and 'To Louisa in the Lane'.

Elegies for friends include 'The Last Signal' (William Barnes), 'The Five Students' (the five people mentioned probably include Emma and Tryphena), 'The Frozen Greenhouse' and 'The Lodging-House Fuchsias' (Mrs Masters). Epitaphs for the war dead include 'Drummer Hodge', 'The Man He Killed' and 'At the War Office, London' (where Hardy says things looked bad enough last year but are now infinitely worse as details of the casualties in the Boer War come in). Hardy also writes an elegy for his dog in 'Dead "Wessex" the Dog to the Household': the former pet plaintively asks whether he is remembered and says he will never come again when called.

Hardy is also his own elegist – perhaps appropriately for a 'dead man held on end'. He recalls memories of childhood (including 'Childhood Among the Ferns', 'The Self-Unseeing', 'Afternoon Service at Mellstock'), regrets the passing of the years (when, for example, he wants to 'Shut Out That Moon' because it reminds him of joys past) and meditates on his own mortality (in poems such as 'I Look into My Glass' and 'Nobody Comes', where he appears as a frail old man in an alien landscape). This elegising tendency culminates in poems where he imagines himself actually dead. In 'He Revisits His First School' he compares his present condition with his school days, regrets returning as an old man to his school and says, 'I ought to have gone as a ghost' (2). In 'Afterwards', Hardy explicitly writes his own elegy and hopes that he will be remembered, if at all, as a keen-eyed countryman.

In 'In a Former Resort after Many Years', Hardy says his 'former mind / Was like an open plain where no foot falls, / But now is as a gallery portrait-lined, /And scored with necrologic scrawls' (7–10). Here is perhaps an explanation of Hardy's compulsion to resurrect the dead: memory confers a responsibility to the dead that can be fulfilled only by writing about them. Memory, then, for Hardy is one of the ways in which human consciousness resists the meaninglessness of space and time. This quotation also suggests that landscape too is inscribed with the memories of the past. For Hardy the only 'meaning' is that which humans project onto the universe, whether landscape or individual brain. And the act of recording these meanings by writing a poem is a further *inscription* and therefore resistance to meaninglessness. The idea that human meanings are projected onto the landscape, and that these memories can be read is made explicit in 'At Castle Boterel', 'The Shadow on the Stone' and 'After a Romantic Day.' In 'Old Furniture', Hardy reads the memories of previous generations in the items that survive them; in 'Beyond the Last Lamp' the human event, the meeting of the unhappy lovers, has left such a strong trace that, for Hardy, 'Without those comrades there at tryst … That lone lane does not exist' (31–3).

Hardy's attempts to reclaim the past in memory are sometimes a way of regenerating the present by reaffirming those human values

 **CHECK THE POEM**
Emily Dickinson's poem 'I Heard a Fly Buzz when I Died', describes a moment which is suspended somewhere between life and death: 'I heard a Fly buzz – when I died – / The Stillness in the Room / Was like the Stillness in the Air – Between the Heaves of Storm'. He copied another of Dickinson's poems, 'I Died for Beauty', into his notebook.

 CHECK THE POEM
In 'On an Invitation to the United States', Hardy rejects the opportunity to go to the New World because it has so little meaning inscribed on it! He prefers to stay in 'ancient' (9) England which is 'scored with prints of perished hands, / And chronicled with dates of doom' (11–12) and enables him to 'trace the lives such scenes enshrine' (14) in his poetry.

which he considered to have been more active in the rural world he grew up in half a century before – a world then largely untouched by middle-class **ideology** and Darwinian science. Hardy felt there was an urgent need to put humanity back into history and the landscape, and in fact the effort to do so shows him struggling with his own feelings of **alienation** – and many poems (such as 'The Darkling Thrush', 'After a Journey' and 'Places') demonstrate that this was no easy task. However, 'The Oxen' nostalgically recalls a time of shared faith and communal solidarity; 'In Time of "The Breaking of Nations"' celebrates the lives and work of country people; and 'During Wind and Rain' suggests that love and fellowship resist time and change.

Finally, writing from the detached stance of a 'dead man held on end' shapes Hardy's characteristically reticent manner, his unwillingness to give too much away even when he is writing about himself and his own life. This is partly a means of self-protection, for Hardy was deeply affected by the controversy generated by the last novels (it is significant that he had doubts about publishing the *Poems of 1912–13* at all). But it is a reticence which is paradoxically eloquent, for in poems like 'The Self-Unseeing' and 'During Wind and Rain' the very lack of specificity gives the reclamation of the past a universal human relevance and force.

LOVE

In his 'Study of Thomas Hardy', D. H. Lawrence expressed admiration for Hardy's novels because the characters are 'struggling hard to come into being … [and] the first and chiefest factor is the struggle into love and the struggle with love'. Hardy demonstrates a similar understanding of sexual love as a powerful unconscious drive in the life of the individual in 'Lines, To a Movement in Mozart's E-Flat Symphony' where the **ballad**-like **refrain** declares that 'Love lures life on'. The 'struggle with love' is a major theme in Hardy's poetry.

Best known perhaps for his melancholic love poems Hardy could also write about happy love, as he does in the complementary poems recording the first meeting with Emma, 'When I Set Out for Lyonnesse' and (this time from Emma's point of view) 'A Man Was

Drawing Near to Me'. More usually, however, Hardy writes about lost love often powerfully and personally felt as in 'Neutral Tones' which places a failed relationship in an incomprehensible universe, or as an observer of another's heartbreak in 'Seen by the Waits'. Related to this are those poems that deal with unrequited love. Hardy's biographers have noted that Hardy often fell in love with women who did not return his affection.

'To Lizbie Brown' and 'To Louisa in the Lane' recall infatuations Hardy had for local girls as a young man. The former, however, shows that Hardy could treat even this theme in a light-hearted way. He gently pokes fun at his own passionate foolishness, ruefully notes Lizbie's dawning sexuality, and concludes by saying that while he remembers her, she has completely forgotten him! Sometimes the object of Hardy's affections was completely unaware of his existence as in 'Faintheart in a Railway Train' where he falls in love with a 'radiant stranger' (6) on the platform he sees through his carriage window, and regrets not getting out.

In the 1890s, Hardy fell in love with Florence Henniker, a married woman of the upper classes. Mrs Henniker made it clear to Hardy that the relationship could never be more than platonic. A number of poems recall this relationship: 'At an Inn', 'A Broken Appointment' (where Hardy says he was doubly betrayed by time and the hard-hearted woman), 'I Need Not Go' (a **sardonic** reversal of the previous poem), 'The Division' (where Hardy speaks of 'that thwart thing between us twain, / Which nothing cleaves or clears, / Is more than distance', 9–11) and 'A Thunderstorm in Town' (when the storm ceases before he can steal a kiss).

Further variations on the love theme include: doomed love in 'Beyond the Last Lamp (Near Tooting Common)' when the unhappy lovers on that wet night made such an impression on Hardy; furtive love in 'The Third Kissing-Gate' when the details of the scene ('the storm-strained trees', 'the gray garden-wall', the woman's 'silent shadow' and 'the hushed mead', 6, 10, 14, 18) leave the reader in no doubt about the illicit nature of the meeting; the fragility of love in 'On the Departure Platform' (a moment never to be repeated); and those moments when love inexplicably fails and is

 CHECK THE BOOK
A comparable male writer of the time with a similar interest in the condition of women was Henrik Ibsen, the Norwegian dramatist, who became established in England partly through Hardy's support. Hardy recognised a kindred spirit in a writer whose work also provoked hostile reaction. One of Ibsen's most famous and controversial plays is *A Doll's House* (1879), which exposes the subservient life of the middle-class wife and mother.

CHECK THE BOOK

Charles Dickens's greatest novels, *Bleak House, Little Dorrit* and *Great Expectations*, explore the predicament of individuals living in an increasingly complex urban and industrial society, but are generally unsatisfactory in their treatment of women, veering rather more towards the middle-class ideal of the 'angel in the house'.

replaced by a dreadful nullity such as 'At an Inn' and 'We Sat at the Window'.

A discussion of Hardy's treatment of the theme of love cannot be separated from a recognition of his contradictory attitudes towards women. On the one hand, he is sympathetic towards the lot of women and has a genuine wish to explore their subjective life, including their sexuality, which is remarkable for a late-nineteenth-century male writer in some ways. On the other hand – **ironically** again because he is a late-nineteenth-century male imbued with the **patriarchal** attitudes of his age – he also idealises and eroticises women. Thus Hardy is aware of female victimisation but also sees women as objects of desire; he wishes to both liberate *and* possess the women he writes about.

The woman who dominates the 'great' love poems is of course Emma and the inconsistencies of Hardy's attitudes to women are brought into sharp relief here. In the *Poems of 1912–13* he seeks to resurrect the young Emma but she is seen almost entirely through the self-reflexive lens of Hardy's guilt and sorrow. Other than in the most oblique references, Emma's sexuality seems to be off-limits. She is a 'phantom figure' (in 'At Castle Boterel', 28), an object of remorseful worship and for the most part silent. She speaks in 'Your Last Drive' and 'The Haunter', and beyond this sequence in 'My Spirit Will Not Haunt the Mound', 'Under the Waterfall', 'It Never Looks Like Summer' and 'A Man Was Drawing Near to Me' but her voice is unremarkable. The idealised image of Emma, a figure who belongs in a landscape of romance, is rather different from the representations of women found elsewhere in Hardy's poetry. They are by contrast stronger, often sexually aware, and less complacent about their status in **Victorian** society.

This different approach is evident in poems which express another, non-romantic kind of love – love for family women. These include 'A Church Romance' (which deals with his parents' courtship), 'The Roman Road' (where he thinks of his mother 'Guiding my infant steps', 13, and not the ghostly Roman legionnaires), and the **elegies** for his mother, in 'After the Last Breath', his paternal grandmother in 'One We Knew', and his sister Mary, in 'Logs on the Hearth'. This latter poem comprises a wonderful tribute to his sister. The logs from the felled apple tree which he and his sister climbed in when they were children now lie burning on the fire-hearth. Hardy poetically resurrects his dead sister and sees her as she was – 'her foot near mine on the bending limb, / Laughing, her young brown hand awave' (15–16). There is a clear reference to Eve and the apple tree here but the Biblical myth is subverted: instead of the weak, transgressing character of the old story the poem presents a vigorous, free and in some ways very un-Victorian young woman who enjoys her physical being.

Indeed, all these family women are presented as strong, resourceful characters. It was from them that Hardy probably acquired his acute sense of the subordinate status of women in a patriarchal culture (a view related to his own lasting sense of class discrimination). These were no 'angels in the house'. Hardy noticed too that women were denied sexual feelings. And he was dismayed by the double standards with which women were viewed at the time: as 'The Ruined Maid' makes clear, women were not permitted the same kind of sexual freedom as Victorian men.

Hardy, then, boldly explores female subjectivity and sexuality – taboo topics in Victorian society – and the victimisation of women. He had attempted this in *Tess of the d'Urbervilles* (1891) with its story of rape, illegitimate birth and adultery, and its frank exploration of Tess's sexual nature. The work was condemned as being immoral and Hardy came to believe that he could explore these issues more freely in poetry. Thus, 'In a Eweleaze Near Weatherbury' a woman's voice frankly acknowledges her sexuality; 'A Trampwoman's Tragedy' explores a pregnant woman's compulsion to tease her lover by flirting with his friend with **tragic** consequences; in 'At the Draper's' a woman whose lover is dying is discovered by him apparently preparing for new sexual encounters as she chooses her fashionable mourning clothes; and the poems 'To Lizbie Brown' and 'To Louisa in the Lane' are both frank about the sexual appeal of these young women. 'The Ruined Maid' ironically suggests that in a society of double sexual standards and where women are treated as cheap labour a woman who sells her body may improve her lot. And 'We Field Women' supports the maid's

 CHECK THE POEM

The Angel in the House (1854–63) is a series of poems by Coventry Patmore which celebrates married love and the Victorian middle-class ideal of the wife and mother. Virginia Woolf, the early-twentieth-century novelist, said women writers should 'kill the angel in the house'.

CHECK THE BOOK

For an illuminating (and indeed ground-breaking) study of Hardy's treatment of female characters in the novels, see Penny Boumelha, *Thomas Hardy and Women: Sexual Ideology and Narrative Form* (Harvester Press, 1982).

argument with its description of the hardships of rural female labour. In 'In the Restaurant' a married woman rejects her self-serving lover's argument for hiding the truth about her baby knowing the condemnation which she and the child will face if the truth should be revealed. In 'A Sunday Morning Tragedy' a mother attempts to secure an abortion for her daughter who dies just as her lover, who initially planned to decamp but who, having reflected on the mother's appeals, turns up to claim her. The story refers to a growing social problem in late-nineteenth-century England: as abortion became increasingly criminalised, and it became more difficult to get a medical abortion, women often sought dangerous alternatives.

Therefore in a variety of ways, Hardy's representations of women in the poems are provocative and revealing. Problems similar to those identified by feminist critiques of *Tess of the d'Urbervilles* are present here too. Hardy may wish to explore Tess's subjective life and demonstrate her victimisation, but he is also in love with her himself. And at the end he destroys her so that no one else can have her. Similarly, many of the women in the poems are dead. Tryphena Sparks, the cousin with whom Hardy may or may not have had a relationship, is the woman in 'Thoughts of Phena, At News of Her Death', and also the woman who speaks in 'In a Eweleaze Near Weatherbury'. Elizabeth Bishop ('To Lizbie Brown') is probably dead and Louisa Harding ('To Louisa in the Lane') died in 1913. Of course, Emma is also dead. As a measure of the contradictory complexity of Hardy's progressive and regressive attitudes towards women, there seems to be an obsessive dimension to his poetic resurrection of dead women. As is the case with Tess, the late-nineteenth-century male novelist who wishes to liberate female subjectivity and desire also harbours a wish to possess the women themselves.

NATURE

Thomas Hardy was a countryman at heart, and he viewed with scepticism the growth of the modern, urban, technological world. It is an oversimplification, however, to say that he viewed the countryside as good and the city as bad. He is quite frank about the brutalities of life and labour in 'We Field Women'; and in 'The

Ruined Maid' the country girl who has gone to the city considers herself better off there. Yet, although in the late 1870s and early 1880s, on the strength of his novelistic success, Hardy had himself prospered in London's fashionable and literary circles, he continued to project himself as a countryman. In 'A Private Man on Public Men' he compares his career with that of his 'contemporaries' (1) who made a name for themselves in the urban world while he was content with the remote countryside, 'Not wishing ever to set eyes on / The surging crowd beyond the horizon' (13–14). For him the city, a place of progress and technological development but also of poverty and despair, is a noisy, troubled place. In 'Childhood among the Ferns' he recalls wishing never to grow up, leave the country, 'And this afar-noised World perambulate' (15).

In 'Afterwards', Hardy implies that he hopes to be remembered as a countryman rather than a poet and the poem confirms this with its detailed observation of nature. The implication in 'Afternoon Service at Mellstock' is that he learned more from watching nature than he did from religious teaching. He was evidently fascinated by the endless vitality and creativity of nature – for instance the natural processes which could turn corpses into new living things.

In 'Transformations' the dead are resurrected in the flowers, trees and grass of the churchyard and 'feel the sun and rain, / And the energy again / That made them what they were!' (16–18). There is a similar idea in 'Voices from Things Growing in a Country Churchyard' and 'Drummer Hodge'. Hardy could be awed by the more spectacular manifestations of nature, as in 'At a Lunar Eclipse' and 'The Comet at Yell'ham'. And as a late-flowering poet, he seems perhaps to have found parallels with his own situation in 'The Last Chrysanthemum' and 'The Darkling Thrush' where against all the wintry odds the creativity of nature is triumphant.

Landscape and the cycle of the seasons provide a major source of figurative language in the communication of theme and mood in the poems. The familiar representation of the passage of time where summer corresponds to youth and winter to age recurs in, for example, such poems as 'After a Journey', 'Where the Picnic Was' and 'Lines, To a Movement in Mozart's E-Flat Symphony'.

CONTEXT

Hardy's sense of the creative energies of the natural world came in part from Darwin who writes famously in *The Origin of Species* of 'a tangled bank [which is] clothed with many plants of many kinds, with birds singing on the bushes, with various insects flitting about, and with worms crawling through the damp earth'. Both writers were aware that there were winners and losers in the natural processes underlying such scenes.

Occasionally, landscape is used as an **objective correlative** for the internal state of mind of the participants as in 'Neutral Tones', 'Beyond the Last Lamp', 'The Voice', 'It Never Looks Like Summer' and 'The Third Kissing Gate'. In 'Wessex Heights' and 'Under the Waterfall' the landscape has a **symbolic** value and suggests the frame of mind of the speaker. In the *Poems of 1912–13* the wild Cornish coast is invoked to sustain the ideal image of Emma.

Hardy wrote many poems about birds. Sometimes this was a sympathetic response as in 'The Puzzled Game-Birds' (can those who rear us also be our killers?) but often it was more than this. Hardy's last three volumes of poetry start with poems that describe country scenes containing birds (e.g. 'Weathers' which opens *Late Lyrics and Earlier*). As well as signalling a new burst of poetic creativity, this is perhaps a declaration that the poet's fundamental perspective is that of the countryman. Hardy was particularly interested in birdsong – probably because for him poetry was itself song. In 'Birds at Winter Nightfall' he actually emulates in verse the song of the bird (as well as expressing sympathy for its struggle to survive in the winter). Birdsong, although beautiful, is a reminder for Hardy of the passing of time: in 'The Selfsame Song' the song lives on but the individual birds die; in 'Proud Songsters' the birds that sing this year are not the same birds that sang last year. Further, birdsong, like the **ballads** Hardy was brought up with (and which had such a profound influence on both novels and poetry), was passed on from generation to generation. Finally, Hardy may have identified with the birds that sing lustily even when circumstances are unpromising: the ageing poet seems to identify with 'The Darkling Thrush' which, though 'frail, gaunt, and small' (21) nevertheless is capable of 'ecstatic sound' (26). The song of 'The Blinded Bird' is particularly striking because it is caged as well as blind. Here there may be a recognition that poetry too is 'caged' by the limitations of a language and though sometimes enchanting can only ever be an inadequate imitation of the original lived experience it seeks to express (see 'A Circular' and 'The Last Signal' where Hardy implicitly raises the issue of betraying the dead by failing to capture their 'sheen', as he calls it in 'Your Last Drive', 16).

CHECK THE BOOK

Hardy wrote in a long tradition of poems about birds. *The Penguin Book of Bird Poetry* edited by Peggy Munsterberg (Penguin Books, 1984) is an anthology drawing upon 1,000 years of English bird poetry.

CHECK THE POEM

In 'The Tables Turned', Wordsworth famously wrote: 'One impulse from a vernal wood / May teach you more of man / Of moral evil and of good, / Than all the sages can.' It was his reading of John Stuart Mill (as well as Darwin) which turned Hardy away from this way of seeing nature.

Hardy knew that it was impossible to view nature in the same way that it had been in former times because of the inroads of modern thought: Darwinian theory had drained nature of meaning. Unlike his **Romantic** predecessors Wordsworth, Shelley and Keats he does not find there an influence for the betterment of mankind. In 'Nature's Questioning' both landscape and animals are seen as like 'chastened children sitting silent in school' (4) who can only speculate inconclusively about the reasons for their existence. Hardy celebrates Shelley in 'Shelley's Skylark' but in this poem the bird 'lived like another bird' (7) and was immortal only in Shelley's imagination. Similarly, in 'Shut Out That Moon', Hardy rejects the Romantic ideal and settles for the reality of his 'common lamp-lit room' (19).

Indeed the country itself was changing under the pressure of a developing technological and industrial society. This theme is a major preoccupation of the novels: the vanity of newcomers to the country is set against the stoical endurance of the country folk. Hardy believed that traditional and customary rural ways and attitudes provided a buffer against the randomness of experience; the vanity of the newcomers made them more vulnerable to 'Crass Casualty' (11) (as he calls it in 'Hap'). In the earlier novels – *Under the Greenwood Tree* (1872) and *Far From the Madding Crowd* (1874) – the rustic characters had had a central role but their influence, and indeed their vitality declines in the later fiction. *The Mayor of Casterbridge* (1886) and *Tess of the d'Urbervilles* (1891) are concerned with the dispossession of country people (both Henchard and Tess are cast adrift in Wessex); *Tess of the d'Urbervilles* also shows a countryside which is being despoiled by the arrival of machinery. In that novel, too, the ancient rituals which had sustained the rural way of life and customary fortitude are seen to be in decline. *The Mayor of Casterbridge* offers the darkest portrait of Dorchester, changing with new developments in the agrarian economy, found in any of the novels.

The treatment of change in the poetry is often less explicit and Hardy casts himself in the role of historian celebrating, but not sentimentalising, the values of country life and work: the stoical endurance of 'Drummer Hodge', for instance, or the folk memory in 'The Oxen', the memories of country customs in 'One We

CONTEXT

The decline of the Dorset **dialect** was of particular concern to Hardy. In an interview published in the *Pall Mall Gazette* (2 January 1892) he said: 'I would not preserve dialect in its entirety, but I would extract from each dialect those words that have no equivalent in standard English and then use them; they would be most valuable, and our language would be greatly enriched thereby.' Hardy, who himself moved between city and country, of course mingles dialect and standard English in his poetry.

Knew', in the seasonal round of country work in 'In Time of "The Breaking of Nations"' and in 'Shortening Days at the Homestead' where the cider-maker arrives with the coming of autumn. The relentless pace of change is sometimes acknowledged more directly – in 'Throwing a Tree', for instance, when Hardy tells us 'two hundred years' steady growth has been ended in less than two hours' (16) or in the references to church restoration in 'The Levelled Churchyard' and 'The Children and Sir Nameless'. 'The Ruined Maid' makes reference to the continuing migration of country folk into the city as well as the decline of the old **dialects**.

In the final **stanza** of 'Old Furniture' (where Hardy traces the memory of previous generations on the possessions which have survived them) Hardy registers his alienation from the modern world: 'Well, well. It is best to be up and doing. / The world has no use for one today / Who eyes things thus – no aim pursuing!' (31–3). This note of being out of joint with an industrial and urban age and its cult of progress recurs again and again in Hardy's poetry. Often the railway is seen as an **alienating symbol** of change as in 'Places' where the 'urgent clack' of the 'vapid' present echoes the train on its tracks (27–8). The journeying boy in 'Midnight on the Great Western', the passenger who sees the 'radiant stranger' (6) from the carriage in 'Faintheart in a Railway Train' and the lover who projects his romantic visions on the railway embankment in 'After a Romantic Day' are all oddly detached from the world around them. In 'On the Departure Platform' love serves to redeem the alienating effects of the 'hustling crowds' (7) at the station, and fellow feeling has a similarly redemptive function in 'At the Railway Station, Upway'. 'The Photograph' describes a peculiarly modern and painful conceit – that destroying an image (in this case that of a former lover) also puts the person to death. And in possibly Hardy's most striking image of alienation, he shows in 'Nobody Comes' the ageing poet in a landscape which includes telegraph and car, the mechanistic and the utilitarian symbols of a world from which he feels remote.

> **CONTEXT**
>
> Claire Tomalin says that a telephone was installed downstairs at Max Gate in 1920 but Hardy refused to use it (*Thomas Hardy*, 2007).

Some poems explicitly question the cult of progress: these include the war poems ('At the War Office, London', 'A Christmas Ghost Story', 'The Man He Killed', 'Christmas 1924' and 'Channel

Firing') and of course 'The Convergence of the Twain'. In the 'Apology' to *Late Lyrics and Earlier* (1922), Hardy argues that technology and war have brought modern civilisation to the brink of 'a new Dark Age'. In 'At a Lunar Eclipse' and 'Wagtail and Baby' he had used nature in both its sublime and humble manifestations to reflect **sardonically** on the activities of humans on the earth. In the former, the spectacle of the eclipse is compared with war on earth; in the latter, the baby observes that the wagtail which is drinking at a ford does not run away from bull, stallion or mongrel – only the (possibly urban) 'perfect gentleman' (13).

POETIC FORM

Thomas Hardy's poetry is characterised by a tension, even a contradiction, between underlying form and surface roughness. This tension can be seen in the way the poems both search for patterns and reflect the disorderly nature of experience. The poems are highly crafted, employing complex **verse forms**, but also containing idiosyncrasies of **diction** and **syntax** and wilful disruptions of **metrical** patterns.

Hardy responded to the charge of crudeness to which these features sometimes gave rise by claiming an affinity between his poetic practice and the design of the great Gothic cathedrals of Europe. These buildings, he said, also recognised the need for fundamental structure but valued spontaneity and freedom as well. It must be remembered that Hardy was initially trained as an architect at a time when the Gothic revival in church building and restoration was in full swing. In his autobiography Hardy claimed, in comments which owe a clear debt to John Ruskin, that his critics had missed the point. Here, as is often the case in the autobiography, Hardy writes in the third person:

> That the author loved the art of concealing art was undiscerned.
> ... He knew that in architecture cunning irregularity is of enormous worth, and it is obvious that he carried on into his verse, perhaps in part unconsciously, the Gothic art-principle in which he had been trained – the principle of spontaneity found

 CHECK THE NET

John Ruskin (1819–1900) was a **Victorian** author, artist and art critic. He wrote extensively on the medieval (Gothic) buildings of Europe and used this work as the basis for a critique of the nineteenth-century industrial and capitalist age. The chapter that influenced Hardy's comments on architecture is 'The Nature of Gothic' in the great study *The Stones of Venice* (1853). A comprehensive overview of Ruskin's life and works can be found on the Victorian Web at **www. victorianweb.org**. Find Ruskin in the 'Authors' section.

in mouldings, tracery, and such like – resulting in the 'unforeseen' (as it has been called) character of his metres and stanzas, that of stress rather than of syllable, poetic texture rather than poetic veneer.

Hardy sought freshness and vitality in his poetry – 'the principle of spontaneity' – and was always prepared to break the rules of poetic decorum in general, and those of **metre**, **diction** and **syntax** in particular ('cunning irregularity'). But this is not to say that he did not continue to believe in *underlying* form or pattern (the poem's 'rational content').

Hardy's views were based on a fundamental conviction that what poetry said (its 'poetic texture') was much more important than the way it said it (its 'poetic veneer'). In other words, a successful poem – one that properly engaged with life – was one which sought to express the 'truth' even if it had some rough edges. Language, particularly written text, that was too polished was liable to become lifeless (and this also explains why Hardy continually strove to create the impression of voices in his poetry). While there is a strong desire in Hardy's verse to discover patterns which might counter the apparent meaninglessness of existence, there is also a vivid sense of the randomness of lived experience. This is the source of the thematic ambivalence which characterises so many poems (see, for example, 'During Wind and Rain').

 CHECK THE POEM

The poem 'Shut Out That Moon' is a **pastiche** of Tennyson showing Hardy's fondness for the earlier poet. In 'An Ancient to Ancients', however, Hardy makes it clear that he rejected the Tennysonian style (see stanza 6).

In rejecting 'poetic veneer' – 'the art', as he describes it elsewhere, 'of saying nothing in mellifluous syllables' – and instead deliberately cultivating an 'irregularity' in his poetry, Hardy was emphatically rejecting what he saw as the 'smoothness' of his **Victorian** predecessors. Writing to Edmund Gosse, Hardy declared: 'For as long as I can remember my instinctive feeling has been to avoid the jewelled line in poetry as being effeminate'. This has often been taken to be an attack on Tennyson. In fact, while he urgently wanted to forge his own style, Hardy admired Tennyson – and sometimes the reader can hear the older poet's influence (as in the wonderful opening line of 'Beeny Cliff': 'O the opal and the sapphire of that wandering western sea'). Hardy's real target was F. T. Palgrave's *Golden Treasury* (1861), an influential, best-selling

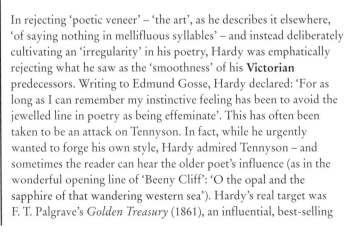

anthology (compiled, it must be said, with Tennyson's assistance) of Victorian poetry. Hardy felt that this volume, with its emphasis on poetry as escapism and its elaborate style removed from everyday language, had disastrously shaped the poetic expectations of a generation.

As discussed in **Themes: The past**, fundamental to Hardy's poetic aspirations is a wish to revitalise the present by recovering the past: together, art and memory could challenge the onward march of time. Hardy was also convinced, however, that memory, and therefore poetic truth, would be betrayed if the representation of the events recalled was falsified by sentimentality, idealisation or, simply, an overly precise treatment. Hardy always endeavoured to capture the truth of the experience he was relating, even if that meant disregarding the formalities of poetry and shocking the reader. (Indeed, Hardy felt he could be even more outspoken in his poetry than he had been in his novels.) When memory is the only antidote to the ravages of time, then accuracy is vital: tidy things up, Hardy felt, and time will always win.

VERSIFICATION

Hardy was fascinated by **prosody** (the study of poetic **metre** and **versification**) and his poems employ an enormous variety of metrical styles and **verse forms**. These range from the sophisticated to the simple, and indicate a continuing willingness to experiment with the raw materials of his craft. The *Poems of 1912–13* are representative in this respect: each has its own distinctive verse form and all display a range of metrical, **rhyming** and other symmetrical effects. But while Hardy uses a greater number of distinctive **stanza** forms than any other English poet, few are totally original ('After a Journey' can probably be numbered among the exceptions). Hardy was a poetic innovator, not a radical, and his experiments were based on a sense of continuity: he continued to favour traditional prosody – demonstrating a particular liking for **ballad** and hymn metres, for instance – and disliked **free verse**. There is no doubt, however, that his experimentation made a significant contribution to the subsequent development of English poetry.

 **CHECK THE POEM**
Hardy's **elegiac** sequence *Poems of 1912–13* is innovative in a number of ways, and this includes the variety of metrical forms and other technical effects he employs (see **The text: Detailed summaries**). Earlier elegies, for example Thomas Gray's 'Elegy Written in a Country Churchyard' (1751) and Tennyson's *In Memoriam* (1833–50), are written in solemn, measured **quatrains** rhymed respectively abab and abba.

Hardy's preference for the traditional forms is nowhere more evident than in his recurrent use of the **ballad stanza** (also known as the short hymn stanza or **common measure**; see also **Ballad form** below). This comprises rhymed **iambic quatrains** – abab – with **tetrameter** a-lines and **trimeter** b-lines. In 'The Oxen' this form serves to enhance the nostalgia for the old days – and undergoes some variation in the third and fourth stanzas to suggest, even at the **metrical** level, how times have changed. Sometimes Hardy modifies the ballad stanza to suit his own purposes. At first glance, 'The Darkling Thrush' appears to use an original eight-line stanza, but a closer look shows that it actually comprises two ballad stanzas joined together. The emergence of a new form out of an earlier one perhaps underlines the poem's modern scepticism, which finds older, more reassuring beliefs increasingly untenable and therefore cannot quite see the thrush as a source of 'Hope' after all.

Elsewhere Hardy uses more sophisticated traditional stanza forms to achieve specific effects. 'At a Lunar Eclipse', for example, is a **Petrarchan sonnet**. The sonnet is in some ways the most regular of forms and its use is singularly apt here, as Hardy uses the form of the poem as an **ironic** contrast to the description of the 'moil and misery' (8) of life on earth. In 'When I Set Out for Lyonnesse', Hardy adopts the traditional form of the **rondeau**. The first two lines of each stanza come round again and convey the young Hardy's excitement following his first meeting with Emma.

On occasion Hardy's poetry is more obviously experimental – most notably, perhaps, in his creation of irregular stanzas comprising lines of varying metrical lengths. In 'The Five Students' there are five separate line types. In each stanza the pattern followed is: tetrameter, trimeter, **pentameter**, a second trimeter, **hexameter** and **dimeter**, all mainly iambic and rhymed ababcc. The effect is to reinforce the **antithetical** nature of the poem, the onward march of life punctuated by the arrest of death, and narrowing to the single survivor (the poet), whose own days are numbered. Elsewhere the different line lengths work together to give the poem a shape on the page which is relevant to its subject or theme. The most striking example of this is 'The Convergence of the Twain', with its three rhyming (mostly iambic) lines (two dimeters and one hexameter)

CHECK THE POEM

In 1798, William Wordsworth and Samuel Taylor Coleridge published a revolutionary volume of poetry entitled *Lyrical Ballads*. It included Wordsworth's 'Tintern Abbey' and Coleridge's 'The Rime of the Ancient Mariner'. Later editions included a preface to the poems in which Wordsworth rejected the **heroic couplets** and poetic **diction** of earlier poets (for example, Alexander Pope) and claimed to use the 'language really used by men' in his poems.

which suggest the image of a ship lying low in the water. In 'Snow in the Suburbs' the variety of line lengths emulates the swirling snow, and the poem finally erases itself – as the snow has covered the street – by narrowing to a dimeter line.

Hardy continued to believe that every poem should have a basic 'verse skeleton' but that it need not conform strictly to this: as long as the underlying pattern was recognised, the poem could depart from it to gain certain effects. For Hardy, this meant above all capturing the spontaneous **rhythms** of speech – not just in **dramatic monologues**, such as 'In a Eweleaze Near Weatherbury', but also in a more general attempt to emulate a consciousness (usually his own) striving to rescue some human meaning from a universe of time and change ('At Castle Boterel', for example) or reflecting on his experience ('The Shadow on the Stone' which has the feel of a private meditation which the reader 'overhears').

Hardy's poetry shows a recurring willingness to disrupt the underlying metrical patterns. In the first stanza of 'After a Journey', for example, the opening line suggests the basic metre is going to be iambic pentameter but it is quite impossible to sustain this reading, as the **stresses** (four to a line, with the exception of line 7) cut across the basic pattern. This is a result of the **syntax**, the strong **caesurae** in some lines, the frequent **anapaests** and the **feminine rhymes** – and it effectively confirms that the poet is indeed 'lonely, lost' (3) as he revisits the sites of his courtship forty-three years before. But what seems strikingly effective to readers nearly a century later seemed less so to many of Hardy's first readers. His experiments, and particularly the disruption of metrical patterns, were widely criticised: many of Hardy's contemporaries were not yet ready for the variations of stress in lines of poetry which were to become normal in the **free verse** of the twentieth century.

A more serious charge, which continued into the twentieth century, was that Hardy sometimes forces his meanings into 'verse skeletons' which are not always appropriate for the mood of the poems. Donald Davie (in *Thomas Hardy and British Poetry*, 1972) claims that this is the case with 'The Going'. Controversially, Davie, who describes Hardy as the 'laureate of engineering' (that is, a

> **CONTEXT**
>
> Hardy may not have shared Wordsworth's philosophy or view of nature as a moral guide but he could agree that it was important to find the language and **verse forms** appropriate to communicate as honestly as possible his 'impressions' of life.

Consider carefully
the rhyme scheme
in 'The Haunter'.
What conclusions
might you draw
from the pattern?
In view of the
poem's theme why
might it be
appropriate for the
rhyme scheme to
resolve itself into a
more regular form
as the poem
progresses?

meticulous poetic craftsman who in this respect can be seen,
paradoxically, as the product of nineteenth-century mechanisation),
finds the poem to be overly symmetrical in ways which 'obstruct'
the developing emotion. Davie writes that what we find is 'the
imperious verbal engineer still, even here, thwarting the true and
truly suffering poet'. Elsewhere, however, Davie – who is actually a
sympathetic and admiring critic of Hardy – concedes that Hardy's
knowledge of metrical form works extremely well in a poem like
'The Convergence of the Twain' (see **Extended commentaries:
Text 1**).

Hardy nearly always uses **rhyme**, often deploying elaborate
schemes, for example, in 'The Shadow on the Stone' where the
pattern helps promote the gentle speech **rhythms** and an intimate,
reflective tone. Hardy favoured repeated rhymes as the foundation
for **stanzas** – a characteristic which gives many poems a **ballad**-like
feel, and the resulting sense that they deliver human truths of value
to future generations, even when they are really not like ballads at
all (as in the case of 'At Castle Boterel', with its ababb **rhyme
scheme**). Hardy often employs **feminine rhymes**, which might be
expected to lighten the poetic mood, but when used in conjunction
with **masculine rhymes** (as in 'At Castle Boterel') can generate a
wistful and moving effect. He uses **triple rhyme** skilfully in 'The
Voice' ('call to me' / 'all to me', 1, 3) to represent the voice of the
woman as it comes and goes on the breeze.

Hardy exploits sound patterning – especially **alliteration** –
throughout his poetry. A notable example is the second line in
'Afterwards': 'And the May month flaps its glad green leaves like
wings'. Hardy regularly uses other symmetrical effects, especially
refrains (as in 'During Wind and Rain') and ballad-like **incremental
repetitions** (as in 'The Five Students', where characters drop out as
the poem progresses). Throughout Hardy's poetry there is a
persistent and conscious wish – reflected in all aspects of his
versification – to find pattern (and therefore meaning) in the
seemingly random nature of experience, while giving due
recognition to the vitality of that randomness. Herein lies the
characteristic tension in Hardy's verse, a tension which confers both
freshness and, often, thematic ambivalence on individual poems.

BALLAD FORM

In both poems and novels Hardy shows an interest in the vanishing folklore of Wessex (see also **Background: Hardy's Wessex**), and especially one of its principal forms, the **ballad**. Hardy wrote many ballads and ballad-like poems. The **narrative** of 'A Trampwoman's Tragedy', for example, is reminiscent of those found in ballads, although the eight-line stanza employed is very different from the ballad **quatrain**. The first four lines of each stanza of 'Drummer Hodge' correspond to the ballad quatrain (although Hardy extends it with two extra lines). Often Hardy's use of a limited pattern of rhyme, which confers an incantatory (song-like) effect on the verse, gives a ballad-like feel to poems which are not ballads at all (a striking example of this is 'The Convergence of the Twain'). Elsewhere the use of a refrain (in 'A Trampwoman's Tragedy', 'The Five Students' and 'During Wind and Rain', for example) echoes the characteristic manner of ballads.

The ballad form appealed to Hardy for many reasons, not just because it was associated with a Wessex for which he felt deep nostalgia. Ballads were probably a greater influence on his poetry than anything written by his contemporaries: in emulating this style Hardy found another way of resisting the uniformity of nineteenth-century, middle-class culture. Ballads sprang from the oral tradition – and this satisfied Hardy's preference for the vitality and variety of speech over the fixity of script (and, indeed, over the 'standardised' English which was beginning to erode the **dialects** of rural England). Moreover, in telling their stories, ballads make considerable use of contrasts (life/death, happiness/**tragedy**, past/present, and so on), and this is echoed in the **antithetical** patterns of Hardy's own poetry – ship/iceberg in 'The Convergence of the Twain', for instance – which were at least in part a challenge to a simplistic, linear, middle-class myth of progress.

The ballad's use of precise but sparing detail and an **impersonal** narrative style accorded with Hardy's own inclination towards reticence – but these characteristics also gave them a universality which he hoped to achieve in his own work. As Hardy realised, however, ballads are paradoxically both timeless *and* rooted in the

> **CONTEXT**
>
> The *popular* ballad has its origins in pre-literate rural communities and flourished in the Middle Ages. Originally a song or orally transmitted poem, a ballad related, through dialogue and action without authorial intrusion, a local story usually of a tragic nature. The *literary* ballad emerged towards the end of the eighteenth century when educated poets such as Wordsworth and Coleridge and their **Romantic** contemporaries adopted and modified the form. 'A Trampwoman's Tragedy' emulates the popular ballad, while elsewhere Hardy employs balladic elements in a more self-consciously literary way.

past. On the one hand, they communicate a shared experience – as Hardy notes in 'In Time of "The Breaking of Nations"', where the 'maid and her wight' (9) are seen to be of more lasting human significance than the 'annals' (11) of the First World War. On the other hand, **ballads** belong to the past – and this gave them a particular appeal for a poet who so often wrote about the passing of time. In fact, unlike traditional ballads, Hardy usually situated his own ballad-like poems in particular times and places (for example, 'A Trampwoman's Tragedy' names several Wessex inns, while in 'The Five Students' Hardy reflects on events in his own life) precisely to underline his concern with transience, the contrast between then and now. At the heart of Hardy's love of ballads lies their identity as stories; it was the ballad form that taught him how to tell stories in both fiction and poetry.

LANGUAGE AND STYLE

In a generally enthusiastic lecture on Hardy's poetry delivered in 1951, Cecil Day-Lewis found fault with the first line of 'Afterwards' – 'When the Present has latched its postern behind my tremulous stay' – because of its odd mixture of the poetic, the archaic and the Latinate, and complained that it was an extraordinarily long-winded way of saying 'when I am dead'. This is a mild (and, in this case, affectionate) instance of the kind of adverse comment that Hardy's language and style have regularly attracted. His choice of words, for instance, is lively and **eclectic**, ranging across – and often mixing – the academic and the **colloquial**, the rare and the familiar, the high-flown and the everyday. Hardy has a talent, too, for the coining of new words and compounds. Moreover, the **syntax** in some poems occasionally displays the same kind of eccentricity found in the **diction**: Hardy regularly employs complex and untidy syntactical structures which can be very confusing, or frustrating, for the reader.

Commenting on Hardy's diction, F. R. Leavis (in an article entitled 'Hardy the Poet' which first appeared in the *Southern Review*, 1940) expressed an academic, and distinctly patronising, view:

If one says that he seems to have no sensitiveness for words, one recognises at the same time that he has made a style out of stylelessness. There is something extremely personal about the gauche, unshrinking mismarriages – group-mismarriages – of his diction, in which, with naif aplomb, he takes as they come the romantic–poetical, the prosaic banal, the stilted literary, the colloquial, the archaistic, the erudite, the technical, the dialect word, the brand-new Hardy coinage.

The charge of insensitivity and ignorance, coming from a critic of Leavis's stature, was very influential but is nevertheless unfair. In part, the odd **juxtapositions** of diction, and (sometimes) awkward word coinages, can be seen as further manifestations of the 'Gothic art-principle' described above (see **Poetic forms**). In large measure, too, Hardy's diction reflects the particular circumstances of his career: a largely self-educated poet, born the son of a rural worker, he was outside the literary mainstream and did not subscribe to any consensus about what constituted a language appropriate for poetry.

So although Hardy often uses some very odd words such as 'continuator' ('Wessex Heights', 15) and 'lours' ('After a Journey', 29), and regularly draws on dialect (movingly in 'The Oxen'), the biggest problem for the literary purists is his tendency to mix familiar and literary diction. An example of this is provided in the first stanza of 'The Darkling Thrush':

> I leant upon a coppice gate
>> When Frost was spectre-gray,
> And Winter's dregs made desolate
>> The weakening eye of day.

This has a self-consciously poetic style: the use of the word 'coppice'; the **compound epithet** 'spectre-gray', which describes the frost (a grey ghost); the implicit **metaphor** in 'the weakening eye of day', which suggests how the sun is diminished by the poor light and the cold weather. But in the midst of all this Hardy uses the homely word 'dregs', which brings to mind tea leaves at the bottom of an empty cup! In the context of the poem as a whole, with its suggestions of how life has been drained from the poet, his fellow

CHECK THE POEM

Like many other poets, Hardy was influenced by Robert Browning's development of the **dramatic monologue** in which a character, not the poet, is the 'speaker' and often at a moment of crisis in his or her life.

CHECK THE POEM

Some of Browning's dramatic monologues are 'My Last Duchess', 'Fra Lippo Lippi', 'Porphyria's Lover' and other poems in the volume entitled *Men and Women* (1855). Hardy's dramatic monologues include 'In a Eweleaze near Weatherbury', 'The Man He Killed', 'My Spirit Will Not Haunt the Mound', 'The Haunter' and 'A Man Was Drawing Near to Me'.

CONTEXT

The mixing of colloquial and literary **diction** in 'The Darkling Thrush' provides evidence of Hardy's position as a transitional poet. In his autobiography he writes: 'The whole secret of a living style and the difference between it and a dead style, lies in not having too much style – being, in fact, a little careless, or rather seeming to be, here and there.' And in this, which really amounts to a rejection of the smoothness of his **Victorian** predecessors, he looks forward (appropriately in this poem) to the poetry of the coming century.

human beings and the landscape – in contrast to the thrush's vigorous song – the word seems perfectly placed to evoke the sombre mood which opens the poem and which is never quite dispelled.

Hardy's word coinages are often rough but meant to revitalise more familiar words and expressions. His particular talent is for the use of **compound epithets**, a technique he learnt from his poetic mentor, William Barnes. They are particularly effective when Hardy turns a keen countryman's eye to the beauties of nature, for example in 'Afterwards' ('Delicate-filmed as new-spun silk', 3; 'wind-warped upland thorn', 7; 'full-starred heavens', 14) and 'The Five Students' ('The sun grows passionate-eyed', 2; 'The home-bound foot-folk wrap their snow-flaked heads', 27). Hardy also had a talent for word coinage, usually by employing prefixes such as up-, out-, over-, in-, en- and un-, for example: 'bedrenches' ('At Castle Boterel', 2); 'outleant' ('The Darkling Thrush', 10); 'unvision' ('The Shadow on the Stone', 19); 'undistrest' ('I Look Into My Glass', 5); 'uncoffined' ('Drummer Hodge', 2); 'inurns' ('Snow in the Suburbs', 14). Occasionally, a new word is generated by the use of a suffix, or in the case of 'wistlessness' ('The Voice', 11), two suffixes – a coinage which F. R. Leavis found to be 'a characteristic eccentricity of invention' (*New Bearings in English Poetry*, 1932). In all these cases, however, a sympathetic reading of the poem in which the words appear can justify their use in the particular context.

Sometimes it is not a question of a new coinage but the employment of the exact – and sometimes surprising – word where, again, the context confirms its appositeness. In 'Beeny Cliff', for example, the use of the word 'chasmal' (10) (the adjective derived from the noun 'chasm') is not a coinage, but its use is sufficiently rare to give it the appearance of one. Similarly, in the same poem, the verb 'bulks' (10), although a perfectly standard usage, sounds odd because it is usually coupled with 'large'. Here, these words effectively denote, after the poem's opening **lyrical** recollections, the poet's change of mood as he returns to present reality.

In a few cases Hardy's critics are perhaps justified, and his employment of unusual words can be seen to have a more utilitarian provenance. For example, the use of the archaic 'Christés' (15)

(Christ's) in 'Channel Firing' seems to have no other function than to complete the line's **metric** form. Equally, the use of 'alway' (8) in 'He Resolves to Say No More' would seem to have rather more to do with completing the **triple rhyme** with which the first **stanza** ends than evoking a particular meaning.

Hardy's occasionally odd **syntax** is often the result of a desire to register nuances of situation or emotion rather than clumsiness. In 'Neutral Tones', for instance, the awkwardness in the second and third stanzas is a matter of grammar and gives the impression of a mind struggling to understand its experience – and revealing strong emotions just beneath the poem's surface. The first stanza of 'Without Ceremony' attracted much negative criticism from contemporary reviewers who maintained it was 'unpoetic'. Here Hardy says that he 'inferred' (5) Emma's sudden departures from home while alive to be the result of her capricious nature. 'Inferred' is delayed to the end of the stanza, which causes much of the syntactical problem, and raises the further difficulty that it seems to be there simply to rhyme with 'word'. Emma's death has prompted him to wonder whether his inference was wrong. (Were there other reasons – including the wish to escape from his hostility – that might explain her behaviour?). The use of the word, and its postponement in the sentence, suggests something of his painful awakening. Sometimes, the syntactical oddity derives from a wish for economy of expression. In 'The Going', for example, the **couplet** 'Where I could not follow / With wing of swallow' (5–6) should properly be 'As with the wing of a swallow'. On such occasions, Hardy risks the general accusation of obscurity and, more specifically, the charge that he has mangled the language to make it fit the poem's metrical pattern.

STRUCTURE

PATTERNS

Hardy's inclination to identify some force which shaped experience (in resistance to post-Darwinian randomness – see **Themes** above and **Background**) went beyond his philosophy of life and extended to an impulse to structure his (considerable) poetic output. This can

 CHECK THE NET

On one of the pages devoted to Hardy on the Victorian Web (**www. victorianweb. org**), Philip Allingham notes: 'Before Shakespeare's time, the possessive form of most singular nouns ended in "es" rather than the modern "s". In the countryside, this old-fashioned possessive continued in use well into the eighteenth century.' 'For Christes sake' was very common in sixteenth-century religious texts.

 QUESTION

Might Hardy then have had reasons other than metrical ones to use the archaic 'Christés sake' rather than 'Christ's sake'?

be seen both at the level of whole volumes and individual poems, and in a desire to find patterns in his own life story which, of course, provided the raw material for those poems.

Most important of all perhaps is the evidence of a wish to order the volumes according to sequences, sometimes placing poems together, on related subjects. Editions of selected poems do not always fully reflect these sequences which include end-of-year meditations ('The Darkling Thrush' for example), poems set in graveyards ('Friends Beyond', 'The Levelled Churchyard', 'Transformations' and 'Voices from Things Growing in a Churchyard'), war poems ('At the War Office, London', 'A Christmas Ghost Story', 'Drummer Hodge', 'The Man He Killed', 'Channel Firing', 'In Time of "The Breaking of Nations"' and 'Christmas: 1924') and philosophical poems ('Hap', 'Nature's Questioning', 'A Wish for Unconsciousness', 'He Never Expected Much', 'A Necessitarian's Epitaph' and 'He Resolves to Say No More'). In the volume entitled *Poems of the Past and Present* (1901) a series of bird-poems, including 'Birds at Winter Nightfall' and 'The Puzzled Game Birds', culminates in 'The Darkling Thrush'. 'The Five Students' and 'During Wind and Rain' are two of three time and journey poems which are placed together in *Moments of Vision* (1917). 'Snow in the Suburbs' is the first of six winter poems in *Human Shows* (1925).

In the later volumes, perhaps because Hardy was getting older and wondered if each publication would be the last, there is a developing pattern of beginning-and-end poems. The last poem in a volume constitutes a farewell – and then Hardy has to make a reappearance in the next volume. His self-resurrection often takes the form of a **pastoral** poem marking the return of spring and usually including birds. Thus 'Afterwards' concludes *Moments of Vision* (1917), and 'Weathers' opens the next volume, *Late Lyrics and Earlier* (1922). Hardy signs off his poetic career with 'He Resolves to Say No More' at the end of *Winter Words*, the last volume (1928).

Hardy's characteristically retrospective mode (see **Themes: The past**) gives rise to the **ironic** counterpointing of past and present which is a recurrent structural feature of individual poems (see, for example, 'The Five Students', 'During Wind and Rain', 'Afterwards' and many of the *Poems of 1912–13*). But in fact Hardy was always keen to discover and highlight **antithetical** patterns in experience, and thematic comparison/contrast can be found in many of his poems – for example, iceberg and ship (in 'The Convergence of the Twain'), Dorset and South Africa (in 'Drummer Hodge'), the human individual and the landscape (in 'The Darkling Thrush'), hills and lowlands (in 'Wessex Heights'). These antitheses, which are evident in the detail (of **rhyme**, **metre** and **stanza**) as well as in the overall structure, are the source of meaning and feeling in many poems. Further discussion can be found in the **Detailed summaries** of the poems mentioned, and in **Poetic form: Versification**.

Hardy also had a desire to find patterns in his own personal story – and of course retrospection aids this. In effect, the main subject of his poetry is Hardy himself and many poems attempt to recount the narrative of his life. Central to this narrative is Emma's death, which prompted the uncomfortable recognition that his love for her was the keystone of his story (this recognition provides the motive behind the *Poems of 1912–13*). The search for patterns in his own life – and in the wider human experience – represents further evidence of Hardy's resistance to the meaninglessness of time and space, and in particular the web of fate which he believed circumscribed all human activity.

POEMS OF 1912–13

Emma Hardy died suddenly at Max Gate, the Hardys' Dorchester home, on 27 November 1912. She was 72 years old, the same age as her husband. Relations between them had not been good for many years – a process accelerated by the publication of *Jude the Obscure* (1895), to which the evangelical Emma objected for both its religious unorthodoxy and its bitter portrayal of marriage. However, her death shocked Hardy greatly. He was consumed with guilt for the way he had treated her, but also experienced an intense revival of the love he had felt for her in the early years of their relationship. In March 1913 he undertook a pilgrimage to Cornwall and the locations of their courtship exactly forty-three years before.

> **CONTEXT**
>
> Hardy's feelings of guilt following Emma's death were accentuated by two manuscripts he found in her room. One was a bitter piece entitled 'What I Think of My Husband' (which he later burned). The other was Emma's memoir, *Some Recollections*, which in many ways inspired the *Poems of 1912–13*. In it Emma recalled her happy childhood in Plymouth, the excitement of horse-riding in Cornwall and her blissful courtship. This document did not contain a single bitter word about Hardy.

The outcome of these events was a sequence of moving poems of memory and grief – even of atonement. For these reasons it is perhaps understandable why Hardy hesitated over the publication of these very personal poems, although they include some of his finest work. The *Poems of 1912–13* are **elegies** but in various ways they challenge the traditional elegiac form – and, indeed, are unusual in a more general sense in that the subject is the poet's wife.

Previous elegies, such as Tennyson's *In Memoriam*, had followed a conventional pattern which paralleled the normal processes of mourning and coming to terms with the loss of a loved one: shock at the person's death, followed by despair, resignation and finally reconciliation. The *Poems of 1912–13* reflect this pattern but with significant variations. The early poems ('The Going', 'Your Last Drive', 'The Walk' and 'Without Ceremony') do follow convention in that they record Hardy's shock at Emma's death. In common with the elegiac tradition there is a refusal to believe she has died; grief alternates with defiance and even irritation (we sense that Hardy is almost asking 'How could you do this to me?'). These poems all deal with the older Emma at Max Gate and with the scene of her death, and show Hardy making initial efforts to come to terms with it. Often the tone modulates into despair.

In conventional elegiac sequences the next stages of the **cycle** show the distancing of the poet from the dead loved one (resignation), the placing of her into consolatory natural processes and finally her integration into memory (reconciliation). 'I Found Her Out There' is one of the most conventional elegies in the sequence. It is perhaps written with less conviction than other poems in the sequence because it goes against the grain for Hardy, with his profound sense of an indifferent universe, to sentimentalise nature as a site where Emma can be reborn in spirit, and partly because Hardy's grief (with its attendant guilt) is too complex to be accommodated by the traditional framework and **motifs**. Indeed, any stirrings of recovery prove to be short-lived. 'The Voice' is undoubtedly the bleakest poem of the sequence and it marks a return to despair. Conventional elegiacs have therefore largely failed Hardy and it is in light of this that he makes the decision to actually go to Cornwall and the scenes of his courtship of Emma.

 CHECK THE POEM

In many ways Alfred Tennyson's *In Memoriam* was the great poem of the **Victorian** age. It consists of 132 connected lyrics and was published in 1850. It is primarily an elegy for Tennyson's friend Arthur Henry Hallam who died suddenly, aged 22, in 1833 – but it also encompasses contemporary anxieties about social change, Darwinian evolution and immortality. T. S. Eliot observed that, contrary to popular belief, it was a poem about 'intense' religious doubt.

However conventional, 'I Found Her Out There' does play a part in the progress of Hardy's mourning: it begins the process of erasing the old Emma and, by distancing Hardy from his loss, it confirms that he is becoming more resigned to her death. The outcome of this is the creation of an ideal **image** of Emma – young, vital and warm – in the core poems of the sequence set in Cornwall: 'After a Journey', 'Beeny Cliff' and 'At Castle Boterel'. Thus Hardy achieves his own form of reconciliation – one which is complex and ambivalent.

There has been much critical debate over the nature of the reconciliation which Hardy achieves in these final poems. Some critics see them as demonstrating how love can conquer time. Perhaps it is safer to say that they are rather more tentative, that they are poems which reclaim those idyllic moments from the past but also record a profound sense of the loss wrought by change and death. And the measure of this ambivalence is the extent to which Hardy rejects the forms of the traditional elegy.

These poems are, as so often in Hardy's work, retrospective: they see a happy past from the perspective of a grieving present. Yet it must be remembered that here the present is doubly unhappy. Love had died between the Hardys before Emma's actual death, as the poems themselves make clear. Thus the anguish of Hardy's bereavement was intense and his elegies are unconventional in that they are guilt-ridden and withhold consolation. This is why the view that love conquers time in these poems is unsatisfactory: Hardy's poetic resurrection of the youthful Emma during that idyllic courtship is qualified by a parallel recognition that she is dead, that things ended badly between them and that nothing can now be changed. 'After a Journey' ends in bitterness, and the final **stanza** of 'At Castle Boterel' sees the aged Hardy bidding a sad farewell to Emma's ghost.

Finally, do these guilty feelings explain why, after attempts to give Emma a voice in the sequence ('The Haunter' and 'The Voice'), Hardy settles for vision? The poetic effort to restore meaning to the landscape by envisioning Emma's presence in it is a perfectly valid one, as it reaffirms the human in a material universe of time and

CONTEXT

Hardy believed that writing and publishing these poems was a form of apology: 'I wrote just after Emma died, when I looked back at her as she had originally been, and when I felt miserable lest I had not treated her considerately in later life. However I shall publish them as the only amends I can make.' Michael Millgate (1985) makes the point that, after reading Emma's bitter comments on him and their marriage, Hardy felt he had betrayed the principle of 'loving-kindness' which informed much of his poetic output.

QUESTION

Which emotions come out most strongly from the *Poems of 1912–13*: love and grief or remorse and guilt?

space. It is no easy task as the enduring, formidable landscapes of these Cornwall poems make clear. But perhaps the ghost's silence is an **ironic** recognition of the failure of communication in their marriage which caused the grieving Hardy so much pain.

PART FOUR

CRITICAL PERSPECTIVES

READING CRITICALLY

This section provides a range of critical viewpoints and perspectives on the poetry of Thomas Hardy and gives a broad overview of key debates, interpretations and theories proposed since the poems were published. It is important to bear in mind the variety of interpretations and responses the poetry has produced, many of them shaped by the critics' own backgrounds and historical contexts.

No single view of the poetry should be seen as dominant – it is important that you arrive at your own judgement by questioning the perspectives described, and by developing your own critical insights. Objective analysis is a skill achieved through coupling close reading with an informed understanding of the key ideas, related texts and background information relevant to the text. These elements are all crucial in enabling you to assess the interpretations of other readers, and even to view works of criticism as texts in themselves. The ability to read critically will serve you well both in your study of the text, and in any critical writing, presentation or further work you undertake.

ORIGINAL RECEPTION

Hardy eagerly awaited the reviews of his first volume of poetry (*Wessex Poems and Other Verses*, 1898). Because he was best known as a novelist, the reviewers tended to be preoccupied with his emergence as a poet and compared his poetic output unfavourably with the novels – much to his dismay. Otherwise, the reaction was mixed. One (anonymous) reviewer's comments are well-known: 'this curious and wearisome volume, these many slovenly, slipshod, uncouth verses, stilted in sentiment, poorly conceived and worse wrought'. The reviewer described the **ballads** in this volume as 'some of the most amazing balderdash that ever found its way into a book of verse'. And he concluded by wondering why 'the bulk of

QUESTION

The critic Peter Widdowson makes the point that the editorial principles for new editions of Hardy's poems vary – sometimes selections are made by theme, sometimes simply according to the order in which the poems were first published. On what principles was the selection in the Everyman's Poetry edition made? Are they anywhere made explicit?

CONTEXT

Reviews of Hardy's poetry appeared in literary periodicals such as the *Saturday Review* and the *Athenaum*. There were many such periodicals in the nineteenth century. Their content included literary articles, reviews and sometimes original writing. By the beginning of the Second World War most of them had closed for economic reasons. The *Times Literary Supplement* continues to review new publications and remains influential.

this volume was published at all (*Saturday Review*, 7 January 1899). However, E. K. Chambers in the *Athenaum* (14 January 1899) noticed the modernity of Hardy's poetry and how it differed from his **Victorian** predecessors: 'There is no finish or artifice about it: the note struck is strenuous, austere, forcible.' In a lastingly influential comment, Chambers said that Hardy's success was limited to a 'small cluster of really remarkable poems'.

Hardy dreaded negative reviews and the ambivalent response of the reviewers continued with the publication of the second volume (*Poems of the Past and Present*, 1901) – sometimes approving, because of Hardy's 'truthfulness' and 'sincerity', sometimes critical, because of the 'harshness' of his style. By contrast, the third volume of verse (*Time's Laughingstocks and Other Verses*, 1909) was received enthusiastically – somewhat to Hardy's surprise. In part this was because of a growing recognition of his skill in **versification**, in part because of the seriousness of his subject-matter as compared to that of other (younger) poets of the time. The reviewer in the *Times Literary Supplement* (9 December 1909) commented: 'again and again throughout the volume is the old sense of the vastness of Time and the littleness of human doings and suffering that gives them a tone of something humbly akin to sublimity'.

Later volumes were greeted with a grudging acknowledgement of their achievement even though both subject-matter and style continued to make reviewers uncomfortable. For those brought up on a diet of Victorian poetry, the fourth volume, *Satires of Circumstance, Lyrics and Reveries* (1914), was altogether too modern. Other reviewers, however, were impressed with this distinctive new voice. From the first most reviewers had concurred that the poems expressed a 'dismal philosophy'. A reviewer of the fifth volume, *Moments of Vision and Miscellaneous Verses* (1917), asserted that Hardy's 'poems are written in a monotony of mournfulness, of dreary and dripping mournfulness' (*Athenaum*, 12 January 1918). Interestingly, Hardy rejected this kind of estimate, saying in the preface to a later volume that his fear was that many of the selected poems were too flippant!

The following years were marked by a growing respect for Hardy's poetry even though some of the earlier reservations remained. For one reviewer the 'harshness' was no longer problematic even though the subject-matter remained so: 'a powerful music is made out of the most intractable material' (*London Mercury*, July 1922). Indeed, by the time of the sixth volume, *Late Lyrics and Earlier* (1922), the more discerning reviewers were beginning to suggest that the very oddities of Hardy's poems were also the source of both their appeal and their power.

By 1925 when Hardy was 85 and the seventh volume was published (*Human Shows, Far Phantasies, Songs and Trifles*), many reviewers commented on the fact that Hardy, now 85, was still writing poems. Normally wary of the reviews, this recognition pleased Hardy immensely. As 'An Ancient to Ancients' suggests, Hardy was very proud of the fact that he retained his poetic energies into old age. It would seem that he planned to draw attention to this by publishing *Winter Words in Various Moods and Metres* (the eighth volume) on his 88th birthday in 1928, but he died on 11 January of that year. As might be expected, for an author who had by now established a national reputation as both poet *and* novelist, the reviews of this final volume were somberly respectful.

In the period immediately after his death, Hardy's reputation declined. He became identified with the rather insipid Georgian Poets with whom he had some thematic (nature, love, the past, mortality) and stylistic (plain language and inventive **prosody**) similarities when powerful new poetic voices were emerging – T. S. Eliot, Ezra Pound and W. B. Yeats. But a centenary celebration in 1940 heralded the beginning of a long re-evaluation of Hardy's literary career which continues down to the present day.

LATER CRITICISM

As the foregoing makes clear, there was from the beginning no critical consensus about Hardy's poetry. There were those who recognised the distinctive achievements of his poetry, as well as those (sometimes expressing the prejudice of a metropolitan

 CHECK THE BOOK
Georgian Poetry was an anthology published in five volumes between 1912 and 1922. Contributing poets included Rupert Brooke, Walter de la Mare, D. H. Lawrence, John Masefield and Robert Graves – although Graves subsequently criticised some of his fellow poets for being 'principally concerned with Nature and love and leisure and old age and childhood and animals and sleep and similar uncontroversial subjects' (quoted in the *Cambridge Guide to Literature in English*, ed. Ian Ousby, 1993).

establishment towards a rural outsider) who found his poems to be both pessimistic and clumsy.

Writing shortly after Hardy's death, F. R. Leavis (in *New Bearings in English Poetry*, 1932) falls somewhere between these extremes. Leavis is at once very shrewd and very narrow in his judgements. His comments can be illuminating. For example, he acknowledges 'that purity of recognition which is Hardy's strength'. He continues by observing that Hardy's poetry 'does what it says, and presents barely the fact recognised by a mind more than commonly responsible and awake'. Elsewhere, however, through a combination of disdain (against a 'Victorian' who had drifted into the twentieth century) and contempt (for poetical clumsiness), he proclaims that Hardy was 'a naïve poet of simple attitudes and outlook'. Leavis's conclusions derived in large measure from a conviction that the important early twentieth-century poets were the **modernists** Eliot, Pound and Yeats, and for many years his judgements were very influential. Most damagingly, he perpetuated the myth that Hardy only wrote a 'dozen' good poems, those being 'lost among a vast bulk of verse interesting only by its oddity and idiosyncrasy' (but he didn't say which ones they were).

In significant contrast to the Leavisites, up until the 1960s it was often practising poets who were most enthusiastic, and most perceptive, about Hardy's poetry. Hardy has had many admirers among English poets, some of whom have acknowledged a particular debt to him. These include Edward Thomas, Siegfried Sassoon, Robert Graves, Edmund Blunden, W. H. Auden, Walter de la Mare, Dylan Thomas, Philip Larkin and Cecil Day-Lewis. In part this can be seen as evidence of the continuing energy of that native English poetic tradition of which Hardy is an outstanding representative (see **Background: Literary background**).

Surprisingly, the American modernist poet Ezra Pound claimed that Hardy was a significant influence on his own work: 'Nobody has taught me anything about writing since Thomas Hardy died' (letter, 30 December 1934). But Pound's admiration for Hardy clearly recognises the ways in which he differs from the modernists: poetry, Pound says, can go down one of two roads, that of 'Music' (its **lyric**

 CHECK THE POEM

T. S. Eliot, Ezra Pound and W. B. Yeats were leaders of the modernist movement in poetry. Eliot was a poet, critic and dramatist; *The Waste Land* (1922) is his most famous poem. Pound's *Cantos* are his outstanding achievement; Eliot considered him the primary figure in the modernist revolution. W. B. Yeats was an Irish poet and dramatist; his most famous play is *The Countess Cathleen* (1892) and major poems include 'Easter 1916', 'Leda and the Swan', 'Sailing to Byzantium', 'The Second Coming', 'Death' and 'When You Are Old'.

forms), or 'The old man's road (vide Tom Hardy) – content, the insides, the subject matter' (letter, 30 October 1934). Thus Pound praises Hardy's poems for their themes (and not treatment, which even he thinks is clumsy) and the retrospective mode in which these themes are delivered ('The old man's road'). Pound could also see that the poetry was, in a sense, the fruit of the earlier fiction: 'Now *there* is clarity. There is the harvest of having written twenty novels first' (letter, April 1937).

W. H. Auden – another poet whose work might at first seem very different from Hardy's – also expresses his indebtedness, but for reasons very different from Pound's. In the essay 'A Literary Transference', which appeared in the *Southern Review*, 1940, Auden says that 'Hardy's faults as a craftsman, his rhythmical clumsiness, his outlandish vocabulary' are obvious but as a consequence he was not an intimidating model to copy. Further, 'no English poet … employed so many complicated stanza forms'. So while Pound says that he was influenced by Hardy's themes and mode, Auden claims that he learnt about form, the mechanics of poetry, from Hardy. But it is an obtuse tribute: Auden somehow fails to see that it is Hardy's idiosyncrasies – even sometimes eccentricities – which confer the power and distinctiveness of his poetic voice.

It was in the 1950s with the work of the so-called **Movement** poets – and in particular the poetry of Philip Larkin – that Hardy gained recognition as the unique representative of a distinctively English tradition, which the Movement poets invoked as a counterweight to the excesses of modernism. Other Movement poets included Kingsley Amis, Donald Davie, Thom Gunn and John Wain. Never a group in any meaningful sense, these poets found common ground in the same honesty and lack of sentimentality, the tone of **ironic** detachment, and the avoidance of any romantic posturing, which are so characteristic of Hardy's poetry. They also shared his commitment to the craft of poetry. Donald Davie was in fact to become one of Hardy's most astute critics (see below).

In an essay entitled 'Wanted: Good Hardy Critic' (*Critical Quarterly*, vol. 8, no. 2, summer 1966), Philip Larkin, a poet who was unquestionably influenced by Hardy, lamented the lack of good

 CHECK THE POEM

W. H. Auden was a poet and dramatist. His early left-wing sympathies are reflected in poetry which is didactic and satirical; later, and following his conversion to Anglicanism, his poetry showed a more Christian emphasis. His influence on other poets was considerable and, like Hardy, he was a master of verse forms. His most famous poems include 'Spain', 'September 1, 1939', 'Lullaby', 'Musée des Beaux Arts', 'In Memory of WB Yeats' and 'Stop all the Clocks' (which featured in the 1994 film *Four Weddings and a Funeral*).

criticism of his poetic mentor even as he asserted his stature: 'Eliot was hostile, Leavis patronising, Wilson, Empson, Blackmur, Trilling – none has been other than neglectful.' He roundly asserts, in a clear rebuttal of Leavis, that 'one reader at least would not wish Hardy's *Collected Poems* a single page shorter, and regards it as many times over the best body of poetry work this century so far has to show'.

Essays by Leavis and Blackmur had in fact appeared, alongside that by W. H. Auden discussed above, in the 'Thomas Hardy Centennial Issue' of the *Southern Review*, 1940, which was published as part of the centennial celebrations. The intent had been to celebrate Hardy's technical craft and poetical prowess. Other contributors were John Crowe Ransom, Allen Tate and Bonamy Dobree. Larkin evidently found some of the praise for Hardy here rather half-hearted but this publication did initiate a modest sequence of New Critical re-evaluations of Hardy the poet, effectively drowned out by the critical clamour centred on the **modernists**, which continued down to the 1960s. At that point two trends converged to bring Hardy's poetry back into the critical limelight. One was the popularity of Larkin's poetry itself in the 1960s and 1970s; the other was the explosion during the same period of Hardy scholarship in biographical and related fields (notebooks, personal writings, etc.). On the one hand, it seemed a good idea to take another look at the poet who Larkin claimed as his mentor. On the other, there were now compelling reasons to examine the autobiographical basis for much of the poetry – a project which the New Critical agenda had effectively suppressed. Examples of important biographical and critical works which appeared after 1960 can be found in **Background: Further reading**.

One of the most influential critics of Hardy of this period was Donald Davie whose book *Thomas Hardy and British Poetry* appeared in 1973. Demonstrating his New Critical heritage with astute appraisals of particular poems, Davie presented Hardy as a humanist writer of 'engaging modesty and decent liberalism' who engaged in a straightforward way with social and political problems and who provided an antidote to the mainstream academic, literary and intellectual ideas of the period. Davie lamented the absence of an agreed Hardy **canon** and the implication was that his thesis would have carried more weight if there had been a consensus as to the 'best' poems: it would be quite possible to choose other poems and come to quite different conclusions! Presenting Hardy as an **elegiac** poet of loss, regret and rural nostalgia, Davie argued that he belonged to a native English poetic tradition which in the mid twentieth century had produced Larkin – a critical view which has proven to be very influential. It should be noted, however, that Davie did not wholly approve of Hardy's role in the development of early twentieth-century English poetry – which he considered to have been more far-reaching than that of Eliot, Pound or Lawrence. He suggests that Hardy's modest poetic ambitions seem parochial when set alongside the avant-garde techniques and intellectual range of the modernists.

CONTEMPORARY APPROACHES

In a provocative and important essay entitled 'Recasting Hardy the Poet' (in *On Thomas Hardy: Late Essays and Earlier*, 1998) Peter Widdowson claims that by the 1990s the Hardy canon which Davie had looked for in vain to sustain his interpretation had been established – not by literary critics and scholars but by the editors of the numerous selections of Hardy's poetry which had appeared after 1979. Widdowson argues that 'Hardy the Poet' has been constructed by the strategies and choices of these editors when assembling selections of Hardy, and that this has been more influential in forming a consensus about Hardy's poetic achievement than any considered interpretive discussion. In this way we have arrived at a central core of about forty 'best' poems which relegates the other 900 plus poems to a lower division! Widdowson suggests that admitting the less well known poems into critical consideration may well encourage us to revalue Hardy's achievement and what constitutes the 'essential Hardy'. Enterprisingly, he concludes his essay by comparing selected canonical poems with other so-called lesser poems, and his interpretation demonstrates that though the latter may not radically change the reader's view of Hardy's themes and techniques, they may significantly reconfigure it.

CONTEXT

Peter Widdowson is a cultural materialist critic. In opposition to the New Critical approach, materialists emphasise that the study of a literary text should be undertaken within its historical, ideological and political contexts. In other words, a materialist is more interested in the conditions of production of a text when examining its meanings than its intrinsic qualities. This approach is sometimes also referred to as New Historicist.

CONTEXT

J. Hillis Miller is a deconstructionist critic, and a major figure in the field. Deconstructionists believe that while texts may give the impression of coherence of meaning this is in fact an illusion: language is a profoundly unstable medium and the search for truth in a text is bound to fail. According to this theory texts can be seen to deconstruct themselves through their internal contradictions. Miller deconstructs both the idea of the literary canon and the traditional view of 'Hardy the Poet'.

The American deconstructionist critic J. Hillis Miller takes this further and says that the whole of Hardy's poetic output should be considered as one *text* where no poem or group of poems is privileged – what he calls the 'essentialising tendency' – over others (*The J. Hillis Miller Reader*, 2005). Viewed in this way, Hardy's complete poems are ripe for deconstructive readings. Miller argues that each poem should be seen as a unique moment articulated in unique language and that this is in fact Hardy's only theme. The poems should not be forced into an interpretive grand scheme which only falsifies readings. Indeed, Miller's position seems to be validated by Hardy's own comments in the Apology which prefaces *Late Lyrics and Earlier* where he says that one should not look for a coherent philosophy in his poems because they comprise a series of fleeting and unconnected moments in time (see **Themes: Pessimism**). Coherence is therefore illusory in Hardy's work, which is in fact a place of discord and discontinuity. Hardy, says Miller, knew this perfectly well himself as he inhabited a culture where the idea of a centre (God) had been erased. From this position, Miller undertakes stimulating analyses of those poems which depend on close attention to the particular 'impression', subjective and ephemeral, which the poem recreates. He examines how the reader resurrects that experience (becomes Hardy at that moment) when the poem is read – and is thereby changed by it forever.

Miller is to date one of the few theoretical critics to discuss Hardy's poetry: his work opens up many possibilities for further study. Much remains to be done, however: Hardy's novels have been approached from just about every modern theoretical position but similar treatment of the poems is largely missing. It is somewhat surprising for instance that there have not been more feminist studies of Hardy's poetry. In the essay mentioned earlier, Widdowson notes that many poems about women, including those where a woman speaks, have not made it into the Hardy poetic **canon** and that the primary image of women that readers have is that of the ideal, and silent, Emma of the great love poems. Reconsideration of the neglected poems should enable a feminist discussion of Hardy's poetry which has been so illuminating in respect of the novels. In particular, says Widdowson, this will reveal the same kind of contradictions in Hardy's treatment of women in the poetry that has been identified in the novels: that is, Hardy is at once sensitive to female victimisation in the nineteenth century but also himself shaped by **Victorian patriarchal ideology**. The contradictions can be glimpsed in the images of female eroticism and victimisation, of independence and ideality in such poems as 'To Lizbie Brown', 'We Field Women', 'Logs on the Hearth' and the *Poems of 1912–13*. This is the same writer who fully understands that Tess is 'constructed' by others (mainly men) but who wishes to possess her himself, as is evident, it has been suggested, when he finally keeps her to himself by destroying her.

CHECK THE BOOK

Both Emily Brontë's *Wuthering Heights* (1847) and Charlotte Brontë's *Jane Eyre* (1847) explore, albeit in different ways, the constraints on women's lives in nineteenth-century patriarchal society and the corresponding yearning for freedom and self-fulfilment.

PART FIVE

BACKGROUND

THOMAS HARDY'S LIFE

Thomas Hardy is perhaps best known as a major **Victorian** novelist. He had written poetry as a young man but achieved literary prominence as the writer of novels such as *Far from the Madding Crowd* (1874), *The Mayor of Casterbridge* (1886) and *Tess of the d'Urbervilles* (1891). In 1895, following the publication of *Jude the Obscure*, he abandoned novel-writing altogether and returned to what he claimed was his first love – the writing of poetry. Between the age of 55 and his death at 87 in 1928, Hardy published over 900 poems and these, by his own account, comprised only a fraction of what he actually wrote.

Hardy was born in 1840 in the Dorset hamlet of Higher Bockhampton, near Dorchester (see also **Background: Chronology**). His father was a builder and master mason, and from him Thomas inherited a love of music; his mother, who had worked as a servant before marrying, encouraged her son's literary tastes. Hardy attended school in Dorchester before being apprenticed at 16 to a local architect. During this period he met and became friendly with the **dialect**-poet and parson William Barnes (commemorated in 'The Last Signal'), and also Horace Moule, who became his literary mentor but who committed suicide in 1873 (see 'The Five Students'). Hardy, an excessively shy but ambitious young man, moved to London in 1862 to work for a firm of architects; he stayed there for five years. During this period he read intensively and wrote poems. He considered going to theological college to train for the Church, but in fact his faith dissolved when subjected to the necessary scrutiny this entailed. The strain of this experience seems to have affected his health and in 1867 he returned to Dorchester, where he again found work as an architect.

At this time he began to write his first (unpublished) novel and fell in love with the 16-year-old Tryphena Sparks, who was regarded as his cousin but may have been his niece. There has been much

---

CONTEXT

Horace Moule was the son of Henry Moule, vicar of Fordington, Dorchester. Moule was an intelligent, sensitive and well-read young man, a freethinker who took a lively interest in the issues of the day. He introduced Hardy to literary, philosophic and scientific texts including Darwin's *Origin of Species*, and Mill's *On Liberty*. Moule's suicide in 1873 probably played a part in Hardy's growing melancholy after this date.

(inconclusive) speculation about this relationship, but whatever its exact nature it seems clear that its failure deeply affected Hardy. In 1868 he went to St Juliot in Cornwall, to undertake the restoration of a church, and met the rector's sister-in-law, Emma Gifford. His first published novel, *Desperate Remedies*, appeared in 1871, to be followed by *Under the Greenwood Tree* (1872) and *Far from the Madding Crowd* (1874). This was his first great success, and on the strength of it he decided to give up architecture, become a full-time writer and marry Emma. Twelve other novels followed and many short stories. By 1880, Hardy was a celebrity frequenting London's literary and aristocratic circles, although often rather ill at ease while doing so. In 1885 the Hardys moved into Max Gate, near Dorchester, a house Hardy had designed himself. Ten years later Hardy wrote his last novel and began to prepare his first volume of poetry.

Why did Hardy abandon novel-writing? He claimed that it was largely because of the hostile reception received by both *Tess of the d'Urbervilles* (1891) and *Jude the Obscure.* (1895). Both novels were condemned as immoral: *Tess of the d'Urbervilles* shocked respectable opinion with its depiction of rape, illegitimate birth and adultery, while *Jude the Obscure* caused further outrage with its treatment of the 'deadly war waged between flesh and spirit'. (In the preface to the 1912 edition, Hardy recounts how the work was 'burnt by a bishop – probably in his despair at not being able to burn me'.) A related factor was the opposition of his wife, Emma, to the publication of the latter novel (she actually tried to block it). Things had not been good between the Hardys for some time but Emma felt doubly betrayed by *Jude the Obscure*: it offended her evangelical religious sensibilities and, in attacking the institution of marriage, seemed to offer up her own union with her husband to public scrutiny. It is possible, too, that Hardy felt as uncomfortable about approval of these later outspoken novels as he did about condemnation. Temperamentally shy and retiring – for all his burning literary ambition – and, **paradoxically**, morbidly sensitive to Victorian proprieties, Hardy recoiled from being seen as a leader of free thinking.

Public and private difficulties, therefore, conspired to plunge Hardy into personal crisis and depression in 1895–6, by which time he had

 CHECK THE NET
A website devoted to 'Thomas Hardy's Max Gate' can be found at **www.thomas–hardy.connectfree. co.uk**. It contains a history and pictures of the house and gardens.

CHECK THE POEM

Hardy read widely throughout his writing career. He studied the **Romantic** poets – especially Percy Bysshe Shelley, John Keats and William Wordsworth, while the Dorset poet William Barnes was an influence from first to last. Hardy also read assiduously the ancient classics paying particular attention to Homer, Sophocles, Euripides and Aeschylus.

become a virtual recluse at his home in Dorchester. Poems such as 'Wessex Heights', and others from this time, reflect his state of mind. Initially, he probably resorted to writing poems as a kind of self-therapy – as well as the fact that he simply enjoyed writing them. But the truth is that Hardy soon came to take his career as a poet very seriously indeed: he subsequently promoted the view that this was the most important phase of his literary career.

Hardy spent hours in the reading room of the British Museum studying the works of his poetic predecessors, one of the fruits of this research being the huge range of **metrical** styles and **verse forms** employed in his poems. He awaited the reviews in a state of high nervous tension and was bitterly disappointed if they were critical, as many of the early ones were (see **Critical perspectives: Original reception**). As volume followed volume (there were eight between 1898 and 1928) his confidence grew and the reviews got better. In addition, the three parts of *The Dynasts*; *an epic-drama of the War with Napoleon* appeared in 1904, 1906 and 1908. This made a major contribution to his rising status as a poet – confirmed when King George V awarded him the Order of Merit in 1910.

Emma died in 1912. The strains in the Hardys' marriage had been evident since the 1870s as Emma's natural vitality jarred increasingly with her husband's reticence. Yet Hardy was deeply shocked by her death and out of his grief and guilt emerged the famous *Poems of 1912–13*. In 1914, Hardy, now aged 74, married Florence Dugdale, who had for some time been his housekeeper and secretary. She was nearly forty years his junior. Public recognition continued to come his way, including honorary degrees from Oxford and Cambridge, a visit from the Prince of Wales, and the Gold Medal of the Royal Society of Literature.

Thomas Hardy died in January 1928. His ashes were buried in Westminster Abbey and his heart in his first wife's grave in Stinsford churchyard, near Higher Bockhampton. In 1917 he had begun his autobiography. This was eventually published posthumously, under his second wife's name, as *The Early Life of Thomas Hardy, 1840–1891* (1928) and *The Later Years of Thomas Hardy, 1892–1928* (1930). This was a curious but revealing attempt to pass on to posterity the 'authorised' (and respectable) version of his life, for it suppressed some uncomfortable personal details (including the relationship with Tryphena Sparks). Indeed, in the years prior to his death Hardy had, with Florence's help, made a determined effort to draw a veil over much of his life by destroying many letters and personal writings.

HISTORICAL BACKGROUND

At the time of Hardy's birth, traditional and customary ways of life were still practised in Dorset, which was as yet almost completely untouched by the incursions of industrialism, or the railway (which did not reach the valley of the Frome until Hardy was 8 years old). By the time of his death in 1928 the world had changed completely: there were cars, aeroplanes, cinemas, telephones, radios – and television had just been invented. The surreal landscape of 'Nobody Comes' in which the aged poet feels himself a stranger includes humming telephone wires and a car which 'whangs along in a world of its own' (11).

However, although Hardy lived on into the twentieth century, his intellectually formative years – the ones which were to determine the characteristic mood of his poetry – were those of his youth and young manhood in the late 1850s, the 1860s and the early 1870s. The earlier part of this period marked the high point of **Victorian** middle-class industrial and commercial civilisation. After the Great Exhibition of 1851, middle-class Britons enjoyed a period of unprecedented material prosperity based on unmatched industrial and agricultural production, and social and political stability. Their buoyant, sometimes arrogant, mood lasted for twenty years, although long before 1870 the factors which were to unsettle that confidence were already taking shape.

Hardy was very critical of this expanding, materialistic middle-class culture, but he was also a man of his time. While he disliked the ethics of capitalism – saying the rich man was usually 'as coldblooded as a fish and as selfish as a pig' – he was nevertheless ambitious himself and hoped for fame and fortune. He hated

CONTEXT

Hardy's decision to write his own life story in the third person, and pass it off as the work of Florence, has met with different critical responses. Robert Gittings (*The Older Hardy*, 1978) found the tactic devious and unlikely to go undetected. He also says that the enumeration of all the celebrities he met is evidence of Hardy's snobbery. Other critics have been kinder – but it is interesting to note that Florence deleted some of the eminent names after Hardy's death as well as several outspoken comments on reviewers who had been critical of Hardy's work.

CHECK THE BOOK

Nineteenth-century Britain: A Very Short Introduction by Christopher Harvie and Colin Matthew (Oxford Paperbacks, 2000) is an accessible account of the complexities of social, economic, political and agrarian change in the period. Hardy's novels themselves, of course, particularly *The Mayor of Casterbridge* (1886) and *Tess of the d'Urbervilles* (1891), describe the changes taking place in rural Dorset.

privilege and the injustices of a class society but married a woman from a class higher than his own and, after his novels made him famous, mixed on equal terms with politicians and members of the nobility. He was dismayed by the irresistible onward march of 'Progress' which was **symbolised** for him by the railway pushing into Dorset and changing forever ancient patterns of country life. But he remained fascinated all his life by developments in industry, science and technology.

Hardy was particularly dismayed by the impact of capitalism on rural communities. Mechanisation was cost-effective and produced bigger crops, but it also increased rural unemployment, and destroyed village traditions and continuity as dispossessed labourers were forced to wander the countryside looking for work. He was acutely aware of what was being lost under the pressures of homogenisation and centralisation. He had ambivalent feelings about the Education Act of 1870 and the introduction of a national system of schooling: this might increase opportunities for rural children but it also accelerated the eradication of the Dorset **dialect**. Resistance to these processes – and, by implication, to middle-class society as a whole – can be found in both the use of dialect and the adaptation of the **ballad** form (see **Critical approaches: Poetic form**) in Hardy's poetry, as well as the recreation of pre-industrial ways of life in both his poetry and his novels.

After 1870, however, **Victorian** middle-class civilisation itself seemed to lose its way. The change of mood was largely due to a loss of economic confidence because of industrial competition from Germany and the USA. Moreover, there were growing anxieties about political instability and social unrest: there was widespread fear of the 'masses' fuelled by violence in urban centres (for example, the Hyde Park Riots in 1866, the Siege of Paris in 1870 and the Paris Commune of 1871). These developments prompted a more general **ideological** crisis which had in fact been simmering away for some years. The fragmentation of Victorian culture after 1870 followed from the crumbling of many of the cherished beliefs – about religion, history, politics, gender, and so on – which had underpinned the successes of middle-class society.

Hardy, as might be expected, was receptive to challenges to the received wisdom of the age, but again, it must be remembered, he was a man of his time and his enthusiasm for the new ideas was, as with many of his contemporaries, not always completely consistent. Thus, like many people after the publication of Darwin's *Origin of Species* (1859), Hardy lost his faith and became a vigorous critic of organised religion and its institutions (particularly marriage), but he retained a religious sense all his life and continued to look to the Bible as a source of ethical wisdom. After Darwin, many Victorians felt themselves to be the victims of time, as it was now difficult to believe that history had a design and purpose (i.e. that there was a divine Providence at work in the world ensuring the triumph of the Victorian middle classes), but while this confirmed what Hardy already felt, he continued to search for patterns in both history and his own personal life (see **Critical approaches: Themes**). In politics, socialism emerged as an active force in British political life after 1880, but although Hardy clearly was sympathetic, he moved in elite circles during his London years and joined no political movement. The nature of women's role in society was widely debated in the last quarter of the nineteenth century, reaching a peak in the 1890s (the debate was fuelled by the 'death of God' and the undermining of **patriarchal** notions, and legislation which improved women's rights). But Hardy's attitude to 'The Woman Question' (as it was called at the time) was ambivalent: while in both his poetry and his novels he does offer sympathetic representations of women, he seems to have retained a very Victorian male tendency to idealise them (as, it might be argued, he does in the *Poems of 1912–13*).

Hardy's quarrel with the middle-class world, then, was genuine if not always consistent. He could be a radical critic of it, but part of him longed to succeed in that world and gain its approval. His social, political and religious ideas led to charges that he was angry, immoral and subversive. But the enthusiasm of other radicals for his ideas made him feel uneasy: one of the reasons he gave up writing novels was that he didn't want to be considered a leader of free thinkers. Hardy valued respectability and this motive informs the authorised version of his life in the 'biography' which purports to be by his second wife, Florence, but which in fact he wrote himself.

> **CONTEXT**
>
> Hardy rarely made his political views explicit in his writing, or anywhere else for that matter, believing that, as Claire Tomalin says, 'a writer was more effective if he appeared open-minded on strictly political questions' (*Thomas Hardy*, 2007). Thus Hardy had nothing to say on the giving of the vote to women in 1918, the first Labour government in 1924, the rise of Mussolini or the emergence of the Soviet Union.

The last vestiges of Victorianism were swept away by major wars: the (second) Boer War (1899–1902), when Dutch farmers fought Britain for control of South Africa, and the First World War (1914–18). Hardy found the 'jingoism' (aggressive nationalism and xenophobia) which was associated with both conflicts repugnant and as a consequence was attacked for writing un-British, unpatriotic poems. He was not a pacifist, however, and supported the war against Germany, hoping that this would indeed be 'the war to end wars'. But his final years saw the rise of the European dictators and in his last poems he gloomily predicted further hostilities.

HARDY'S WESSEX

CHECK THE NET

Maps of Hardy's Wessex, including his own 1895 map, can be found on the Thomas Hardy web page, **www.yale.edu/ hardysoc**. Click on 'Images of Hardy Country'.

'Wessex Heights' is often seen as the poem which marks Hardy's renunciation of novel-writing and commitment to poetry following the uproar which greeted *Jude the Obscure* (1895) (see **Thomas Hardy's life** above). The four hills named in this poem mark out, approximately, the ancient kingdom of Wessex which Hardy uses as the setting for most of his novels and many of his poems. Hardy's fictionalised Wessex is centred on Dorset, and particularly Dorchester (which he called 'Casterbridge'). Wessex first appears in *Far from the Madding Crowd* (1874), and its topography is fully delineated in subsequent novels. In 'Wessex Heights', Hardy announces that the region will also be his poetic domain.

Historically, Wessex was one of the seven kingdoms of the Anglo-Saxons (specifically, the territory of the West Saxons) following Britain's separation from the Roman Empire around AD 500. It probably covered the present-day counties of Hampshire, Dorset, Wiltshire, Berkshire, Somerset and Devon, and its main centres were Winchester and Southampton. Wessex reached the height of its power in the tenth century (by now including Kent and Sussex) after the rule of its best-known king, Alfred the Great. Alfred was alone amongst the Anglo-Saxon kings in successfully resisting the raids of the Vikings; his successors fought to regain the land the Vikings had conquered (the 'Danelaw') and eventually united all England (literally 'land of the Angles') under a single monarchy in AD 954.

For Hardy, though, Wessex was as much a landscape of the mind as it was a place with a social and historical reality. He himself said that Wessex was 'partly real, partly dream'. In many ways a **symbolic** landscape, it represented Hardy's sense of the inexorable passage of time (in both its long, many-layered history as well as Hardy's personal experiences) and the indifference of nature (a place where generations of transient human beings, including his own family, had lived and died). It was a site, then, where past and present rubbed against each other, where human vulnerability was continually reiterated (the sources of **alienation**) – but where community life and individual memory (the patterning impulses of consciousness) offered resistance to the bleak and meaningless realities of space and time. In this respect, Hardy's imagined Wessex externalised his mental landscape.

This is not to say, however, that Hardy was not acutely aware of the real problems of contemporary Wessex. He felt a genuine fellowship with agricultural workers – this is reflected in 'Drummer Hodge', where the **elegiac** form of the poem itself challenges those class attitudes which had led to a scandalous neglect of rural hardship. Above all, perhaps, Hardy saw himself as a historian of a valued, and ancient, way of life in a region which was being disrupted by nineteenth-century social and economic change (see **Historical background** above). Thus in the poems we find a wish to record for posterity details, both personal and public, of that threatened culture: family traditions ('The Self-Unseeing'), folk-tales ('The Oxen'), the Dorsetshire **dialect** ('The Ruined Maid') as well as, more generally, the recurring patterns of rural life and work ('In Time of "The Breaking of Nations"' and 'During Wind and Rain').

Hardy understood the dangers of this kind of commemoration of a disappearing Wessex – specifically, the temptation to romanticise the region for a sophisticated, and largely urban, readership (on whom, after all, he depended for his livelihood). Indeed, this kind of criticism has been levelled at the portrayal of Wessex in his novels. However, Hardy actively resists this charge in his poems, where, as has been suggested, he felt able to express his real opinions more freely: in a poem such as 'The Darkling Thrush',

CHECK THE BOOK

In an essay entitled 'Wessex' in *The Cambridge Companion to Thomas Hardy* (1999), ed. Dale Kramer, Simon Gatrell says that the idea of Wessex evolved in Hardy's imagination as the novels appeared and is really only fully developed in the last three. Moreover, another reason Hardy ceased novel-writing, suggests Gatrell, was a growing awareness that the old Wessex, and therefore the locale for the novels, was disappearing: in the poetry Wessex becomes exclusively a landscape of the mind (and this is in part what 'Wessex Heights' is all about).

for example, he is quite uncompromising in his depiction of the harsher aspects of Wessex and a landscape which is merely 'haunted' by humankind (7).

LITERARY BACKGROUND

W. H. Auden said of Hardy that 'he was modern without being too modern', an ambivalence which highlights the difficulty in placing Hardy in literary history. Born in 1840, Hardy might seem to be in origin a **Victorian** (although the accident of birth isn't necessarily a sound basis for determining literary classification). Latterly he was a contemporary of the **modernist** poets T. S. Eliot, Ezra Pound and W. B. Yeats, and novelists James Joyce, D. H. Lawrence and Virginia Woolf – who were at the height of their powers while he was still alive. In his later years, Hardy kept abreast of new developments in literature. He read D. H. Lawrence's poems though apparently not the novels, corresponded with Ezra Pound, and talked with Virginia Woolf – while seeing himself as a 'survivor of an almost extinct species' and a 'mid-Victorian relic'.

So, in literary terms, to what extent is it appropriate to speak of Hardy as a Victorian? What evidence is there of modernism in his work both fiction and poetry? Is it better to think of him as a transitional figure between literary periods? Or should we attempt to formulate a quite different way of placing Hardy – one which is somewhat outside the mainstream literary movements and accepted critical categories?

THE NOVELIST

When Hardy's first novel was published (*Desperate Remedies*, 1871) the novel was the dominant literary form of the age. In later years Hardy was to claim, perhaps retrospectively, that poetry was his first love and that he wrote novels because he had to earn a living. But, because the poet emerged from the novelist, a brief examination of Hardy's relationship to the development of the nineteenth-century novel sheds light on his status as a poet. Literary historians have tended to place Hardy the novelist in the mainstream of nineteenth-century realist fiction and there is a clear

CHECK THE BOOK

On the strength of *Middlemarch* (1871–2) many contemporaries considered George Eliot the greatest novelist of the Victorian age, a view endorsed by F. R. Leavis in the twentieth century.

debt to George Eliot (especially perhaps in her earlier novels such as *Adam Bede*, 1859). Yet Hardy's novels are rather unlike those of his illustrious predecessors – and indeed his immediate contemporaries – in terms of both style and subject-matter.

It is perhaps more accurate to say that in the novels Hardy seeks to combine realism with the sensational – through the examination of rural social change coupled with extravagant plots often dependent on coincidence and chance. Indeed towards the end of the century when the ongoing nineteenth-century debate about the merits in fiction of realism or romance was sharpened by the emergence of the so-called 'new realists' (George Moore, George Gissing and Arnold Bennett) and a corresponding revival of romance (Robert Louis Stevenson) it is perhaps more appropriate to place Hardy in the latter camp. In a statement which is as applicable to the poetry as the novels, Hardy says in his autobiography: 'Art consists in so depicting the common events of life as to bring out the features which illustrate the author's idiosyncratic mode of regard; making old incidents and things seem as new.' Here Hardy defends the validity of the personal view in ways which are reminiscent of his description of his poems as 'fugitive impressions' of life. Thus, while Hardy sought a degree of modern impersonality in his work he continued to endorse an older (and **Romantic**) belief in the capacity of art to express the unique mind and personality of the artist.

For Hardy this meant first and foremost telling stories, however improbable, which engaged the imagination of the reader. Of the realism of such writers as Moore, Gissing and Bennett he said: 'They forget in their insistence on life, and nothing but life, in a plain slice, that *a story must be worth the telling*, that a good deal of life is not worth any such thing, and that they must not occupy a reader's time with what he can get at first hand anywhere around him.' Elsewhere he says bluntly: 'Realism is not art.' Hardy thought of himself as a story-teller, and his plots were shaped by the **ballads** of love and betrayal he had heard as a boy. In this respect too it has been observed that many of the poems have a strong **narrative** element. Indeed, John Bayley once said that '*all* Hardy's poems are sung short stories'. And, conversely, it has often been pointed out

CHECK THE BOOK

George Moore's novels include *A Modern Lover* (1883) and *Esther Waters* (1894). George Gissing is best known for *The Nether World* (1889) and *New Grub Street* (1891), novels which focus on poverty and failure in the slums of late-nineteenth-century London. Arnold Bennett's novels include *Anna of the Five Towns* (1902) and *The Old Wives Tale* (1908), while Robert Louis Stevenson wrote *Treasure Island* (1883) and *The Strange Case of Dr Jekyll and Mr Hyde* (1886).

THE NOVELIST continued

CHECK THE BOOK

Both Gustave Flaubert's *Madame Bovary* (1857) and Leo Tolstoy's *Anna Karenina* (1873–7) deal with the desires and longings of young women who feel frustrated by the constraints of their social environments. Emma Bovary has been compared with Eustacia Vye in *The Return of the Native* (1878) but whereas Emma is mercilessly analysed, Eustacia's spirit is celebrated. In novels like *Germinal* (1885) and *La Bête Humaine* (The Beast in Man, 1890), Emile Zola depicts characters sunk in a nightmare of poverty, drink, sexual obsession and insanity.

that the latent poet is evident in the novels: description and imagery, and indeed the overall conception of the novels, have poetic qualities.

If stylistically Hardy diverged from his novel-writing contemporaries, then the same could be said of his subject-matter. In particular it was Hardy's outspokenness about sexual love which set him apart from other nineteenth-century novelists and attracted so much criticism. The Brontës had found covert ways of talking about women's sexual lives as had George Eliot later in the century; Dickens by contrast carefully avoided such material so as not to offend the sensibilities of his middle-class readership. Indeed, Hardy's contemporaries saw more resemblance in this respect between him and the great European novelists Flaubert, Tolstoy and Zola. But Hardy did not approve of the sexual sensationalism of the naturalist writers. In fact he was dismayed that his novels were being condemned while Zola seemed to be enjoying more licence, and he was appalled when Margaret Oliphant, a minor novelist, damned *Jude the Obscure* (1895) for being Zolaesque. In the 1890s he came to the conclusion that poetry afforded more opportunities to challenge sexual and religious convention than did fiction.

The early twentieth-century writer who has the most in common with Hardy is D. H. Lawrence. They shared the post-Darwinian belief in what Hardy calls in *Jude the Obscure* (1895) 'the war between flesh and spirit', in other words a recognition that human beings may have fine aspirations arising from a sense of freedom and the possibility of choice but are also subject to the forces of nature or unconscious drives – above all, the sexual drive. In his 'Study of Thomas Hardy' (which is rather more about his own beliefs than Hardy's fiction), Lawrence comments on the energy displayed by Hardy's characters – which he thought rather subverted the common view that Hardy was pessimistic – saying that they are 'struggling hard to come into being ... [and that] the first and chiefest factor is the struggle into love and the struggle with love'. This of course was a central theme of Lawrence's novels too.

Lawrence rejected what he called the 'old stable ego of character' in the novel on which the **Victorian** novel had been based, that is the representation of human beings in their social aspect and relationships, and sought to explore the inner life. The publication in 1914 of James Joyce's *Portrait of the Artist as a Young Man* and *Dubliners* confirmed that the notion of the essentialism of character which could be confidently described was now outmoded. Hereafter, as Joyce showed in his development of the 'stream of consciousness' technique, 'personality' was understood to be a shifting and unstable entity. In his novels, Hardy had for the most part accepted the conventional idea of the unity of character and in this sense perhaps *does* belong in the mainstream of nineteenth-century realist fiction (*Tess of the d'Urbervilles* is probably the exception as the eponymous heroine is constructed from multiple viewpoints: she *is* what others wish to make of her.) However, Hardy's poetry, by his own admission comprising 'fugitive impressions', 'questionings' of reality and explorations of his own inner life, in many ways anticipates the experimental fiction of the modernists Joyce, Lawrence and Woolf.

THE POET

There is little evidence that Hardy's poetic practice or theory was significantly influenced by other Victorian poets. However, his extensive reading and research resulted in poems which contain numerous references and **allusions** to other poets, both of the nineteenth century and earlier. Critics have pointed out particular debts to Robert Browning, whose tough-minded philosophical poetry, interest in history and exploitation of the **dramatic monologue** appealed to Hardy. Similarly, Tennyson's **elegiac** style and melancholy reflections on the passage of time may have played some part in shaping Hardy's characteristic manner.

Often one feels that it is other writers' *ideas* rather than their practice which have the most influence on Hardy's work – which, in terms of style, remains idiosyncratically his own. For example, Hardy admired Swinburne's 'musical' poetry – but seems to have been even more impressed by his unconventional ideas on religion, politics and sex (notably, a very un-Victorian interest in passion). Hardy shared Swinburne's pessimism: both writers thought that the universe was indifferent to human hopes and aspiration and that the only hope for betterment lay in the collective efforts of humankind.

CHECK THE BOOK

D. H. Lawrence's novels – *Sons and Lovers* (1913), *The Rainbow* (1915), *Women in Love* (1920) and *Lady Chatterley's Lover* (which was not published in an unexpurgated edition until 1960) – outraged public opinion largely because of their sexual frankness. Like Hardy's, his poetry moved beyond the formalism of his predecessors without fully embracing a **modernist** style.

CHECK THE BOOK

Virginia Woolf developed the 'interior monologue' and is regarded as one of the great innovative novelists of the twentieth century. Her best known novels include *Mrs Dalloway* (1925), *To the Lighthouse* (1927) and *The Waves* (1931).

THE POET continued

CHECK THE POEM

A. C. Swinburne's lyric poems are evident in the verse drama *Atlanta in Calydon* (1865), an attempt to emulate the form and style of ancient Greek tragedy. The volume *Poems and Ballads* (1866) contains some of his finest poems including 'Dolores' and 'The Garden of Proserpine'. Hardy was impressed by the variety of verse forms Swinburne employed. Others sometimes felt that Swinburne's creation of poetic melody often meant the sacrifice of meaning – F. R. Leavis and T. S. Eliot thought his influence on later poets had been disastrous.

Hardy also felt that Swinburne had been treated harshly by public opinion, just like himself (see **Thomas Hardy's life** above on the reception of his last two novels).

On the other hand, some critics have endeavoured to find traces of **modernism** in Hardy's poetry, saying that it evinces anti-Victorian tendencies everywhere, in style as well as theme. Ezra Pound found specifically **imagist** qualities in Hardy's work, and critics point to 'Snow in the Suburbs' as the best example of this. Others have found a more general modernist flavour in Hardy's deliberate disruption of **metrical** patterns, his **syntactic** eccentricities, his **neologisms**, his mixing of **colloquial** and literary **diction**, his sudden shifts in tone and so on – in other words, all those stylistic features which constitute Hardy's idiosyncrasy (see **Critical approaches: Poetic form**). Hardy distrusted written language for the same reason as the modernists, fearing that it might slide into lifeless fixity; he sought to give his poems an asymmetry which would preserve their freshness.

It has also been suggested that Hardy echoes the anti-**Romantic** stance of the modernists. Eliot, Pound and Yeats all endeavoured to write **impersonally**, from perspectives not necessarily their own. They rejected the Wordsworthian **egotistical sublime** where a poet's preoccupation with his or her own life, thoughts and feelings is the very essence of the poet's work. One might object that this is precisely why T. S. Eliot had so little time for Hardy, a writer who seems to have accepted that the proper subject of his poetry was his own life. Yet, as shown in **The text: Detailed summaries**, although Hardy writes out of his own experience, he does so with a surprising degree of reticence that prevents the reader getting close to him. This seems to have much in common with Yeats's adoption of masks, in poems akin to **dramatic monologues** where the speaker is clearly not the poet, or Eliot's assumption of different **personae** in *The Waste Land* (1922). Thus Hardy shares the modernist suspicion of Romantic soul-bearing.

The problem with this is that although Hardy may be to some extent arguing with his Romantic inheritance – in ways which give his poetry a modernist flavour – there are other ways in which his debt to the Romantics (Shelley, Keats and in particular Wordsworth) is clear. Hardy shared Wordsworth's view expressed in the Preface to the 1800 edition of *Lyrical Ballads* that the language proper to poetry is the 'real language of men' – and both writers shared an enthusiasm for **ballads**. Both wrote their poetry out of personal memory (though Wordsworth wrote about his childhood while Hardy recalled his young manhood and days of courtship). Both showed in their poems an affinity for the natural world (though Wordsworth's pantheistic universe, i.e. one where God is present in all things, is replaced in Hardy by an indifferent one). Both writers valued the representation of endurance in humans as a response to the unpredictability of life.

When T. S. Eliot, and some twentieth-century critics, label Hardy a 'Victorian' they do so because of the Romantic qualities of his writing. But they fail to see that his debt bypasses Victorian corruptions of Romanticism (which was their real target) and goes back to the source in Wordsworth himself. In the light of this, it is much more illuminating to think of Hardy's poetry as belonging to a distinctively native English poetic tradition which is neither Victorian nor modernist, which includes Wordsworth, but also poets like John Clare, and has its origins in folk poetry and folk-songs. This indigenous tradition was effectively suppressed during the Victorian period, and prior to Hardy surfaces mainly in the works of William Barnes, the Dorset **dialect**-poet (who knew Hardy personally), and sometimes in Tennyson.

Identifying the features of this native English tradition provides a useful guide to the essential characteristics of Hardy's poetry. It deals with ordinary, everyday experience (the 'maid and her wight', rather than 'War's annals', as 'In Time of "The Breaking of Nations"' puts it). It is restrained in its treatment and uses the 'real language of men'. It assumes a universality of thoughts and feelings – a contentious notion by the end of the twentieth century, but surely exemplified in poems like 'The Self-Unseeing'. In any discussion of Hardy's place in a native tradition it is important to recall that his poetry is rooted in the ballad form (see **Critical approaches: Poetic form**).

 CHECK THE POEM

John Clare's first published volume was *Poems Descriptive of Rural Life and Scenery* (1820). His best poems, which include 'Remembrances' and 'Decay', are similar to Hardy's in that they deal with lost love and the decline of rural communities and an ancient way of life.

CHECK THE POEM

T. S. Eliot's 'The Love Song of J. Alfred Prufrock' (1915) is a **dramatic monologue** in the style of Robert Browning, although its modernist 'stream-of-consciousness' style, complex **allusions** and **symbolism** are very different from anything Hardy wrote. Prufrock's disillusionment with modern society, his frustrations in love, and his preoccupation with personal ageing and decay are all themes which can be found in Hardy's poetry, however.

While seeing Hardy as a key figure in a native English poetic tradition (see **Critical perspectives** for further discussion), it is still perfectly valid to regard Hardy the poet as a transitional figure between **Victorian** and **modernist** literature. The awareness of human beings as the victims of time and history, which grew in the nineteenth century and is a major theme in Hardy's poetry, is perhaps an even more intense preoccupation of a twentieth-century writer like T. S. Eliot.

World events	Author's life	Literary events
1831–6 Charles Darwin works as unpaid naturalist aboard HMS *Beagle*		
	1832 Birth of Horace Moule	
1837 Queen Victoria succeeds William IV		
1840 Marriage of Queen Victoria and Prince Albert	**1840** Birth of Hardy at Higher Bockhampton, Dorset, on 2 June; birth of Emma Lavinia Gifford	**1840** Robert Browning, *Sordello*
		1842 Alfred, Lord Tennyson, *Poems*
		1844 William Barnes, *Poems of Rural Life in the Dorset Dialect*
1847 Railway reaches Dorchester		**1847** Charlotte Brontë, *Jane Eyre*; Emily Brontë, *Wuthering Heights*
1848 Revolutionary uprisings throughout mainland Europe	**1848–9** Attends village school in Lower Bockhampton	
	1850–3 Educated at Isaac Last's British School (Nonconformist) in Dorchester	**1850** Death of William Wordsworth; Tennyson, *In Memoriam*
1851 The Great Exhibition is held at the Crystal Palace in London		
	1853–6 Attends Isaac Last's new Congregationalist 'Academy'; starts learning Latin	**1853** Charles Dickens, *Bleak House*
1854–6 Crimean War		
		1855 Browning, *Men and Women*

World events

1859 Darwin publishes *On the Origin of Species*

1870 Forster's Elementary Education Act sets up school boards in Britain

1871 Darwin publishes *The Descent of Man*

Author's life

1856 Apprenticed to ecclesiastical Dorchester architect John Hicks; meets dialect-poet William Barnes

1857 Meets Horace Moule; begins to write poetry

1862 Moves to London to work as an assistant architect for Arthur Blomfield

1865 Abandons plan to train for the Church due to religious doubts

1867 Returns to Dorchester to work for Hicks again; forms relationship with Tryphena Sparks

1869 Works as architect for G. R. Crickmay in Weymouth; possibly engaged to Tryphena Sparks

1870 Meets Emma Gifford while on architectural business in St Juliot, Cornwall; moves to London again to pursue career as architect

1871 Publication of *Desperate Remedies*; returns to Weymouth to work as architect; trips to Cornwall

Literary events

1857 Gustave Flaubert, *Madame Bovary*

1859 George Eliot, *Adam Bede*

1860 Browning, *Dramatis Personae*

1865 Algernon Charles Swinburne, *Atalanta in Calydon*; birth of William Butler Yeats

1866 Swinburne, *Poems and Ballads*

1867 Matthew Arnold, *New Poems*

1869 Arnold, *Culture and Anarchy*; Tennyson, *The Holy Grail and Other Poems*

1871 Swinburne, *Songs before Sunrise*

World events	Author's life	Literary events
	1872 Works as architect in London; publishes *Under the Greenwood Tree*	
	1873 Publication of *A Pair of Blue Eyes*; becomes engaged to Emma; Moule commits suicide in Cambridge	
	1874 Marriage to Emma; decides to become full-time writer following success of *Far from the Madding Crowd*	
	1876 Publication of *The Hand of Ethelberta*	**1876** Lewis Carroll, *The Hunting of the Snark*
	1876–8 Lives in Sturminster Newton	
1877 Queen Victoria assumes the title of Empress of India; Thomas Edison invents the phonograph		
	1878 Publishes *The Return of the Native*; becomes a figure on the London literary scene	
1879 Edison produces incandescent electric light	**1879** Birth of Florence Emily Dugdale	**1879** Henrik Ibsen, *A Doll's House*
1880–1 First Boer War in southern Africa, ending in defeat for the British	**1880–1** Publication of *The Trumpet Major*; bedridden, dictates *A Laodicean* to Emma	**1880** Tennyson, *Ballads and Other Poems*
1882 Death of Charles Darwin	**1882** Attends Darwin's funeral; publication of *Two on a Tower*	**1882** Swinburne, *Tristram of Lyonesse and Other Poems*
	1883 Moves to Dorchester; publishes *The Dorsetshire Labourer*	**1883** George Moore, *A Modern Lover*
	1885 Moves into Max Gate (the house Hardy had designed himself)	**1885** Birth of Ezra Pound; Emile Zola, *Germinal*

World events	Author's life	Literary events
	1886 Publication of *The Mayor of Casterbridge*; begins to plan epic *The Dynasts* about the Napoleonic Wars	**1886** Robert Louis Stevenson, *The Strange Case of Dr Jekyll and Mr Hyde*
	1887 Publication of *The Woodlanders*; visits Italy	**1887** George Meredith, *Ballads and Poems of Tragic Life*
1888 'Jack the Ripper' murders terrorise East London	**1888** Collection of short stories published as *Wessex Tales*	**1888** Birth of T. S. Eliot; death of Arnold
		1889 Death of Robert Browning
	1890 Death of Tryphena Sparks	
1891 Assisted Education Act makes elementary education free in Britain	**1891** Success and financial security follow *Tess of the d'Urbervilles*; marriage begins to deteriorate	**1891** George Gissing, *New Grub Street*
	1892 Death of Thomas Hardy's father; publishes *The Well-Beloved* in serial form	**1892** Death of Tennyson
	1893 Meets Florence Henniker in Dublin and becomes infatuated	
	1894 Publishes the collection of stories *Life's Little Ironies*	**1894** George Bernard Shaw, *Mrs Warren's Profession*
	1895 Public outrage follows publication of *Jude the Obscure*; marriage increasingly unhappy	**1895** Yeats, *Poems*; birth of Robert Graves
	1896 Abandons novels after reception of *Jude the Obscure*; devotes himself to poetry	**1896** A. E. Housman, *A Shropshire Lad*; birth of Edmund Blunden
	1898 Publishes *Wessex Poems and Other Verses*	**1898** Oscar Wilde, *The Ballad of Reading Gaol*

World events	Author's life	Literary events
	1899 Publishes *Poems of the Past and Present*	**1899** Yeats, *The Wind Among the Reeds*
		1902 Arnold Bennett, *Anna of the Five Towns*
	1904 First volume of *The Dynasts* appears; meets Florence Dugdale; death of Thomas Hardy's mother	
	1906 Publication of *The Dynasts, Part II*	
		1907 Birth of W. H. Auden
	1908 Publication of *The Dynasts, Part III*	**1908** Yeats, *Collected Works*
	1909 Publishes *Time's Laughingstocks and Other Verses*; succeeds George Meredith as President of the Society of Authors	**1909** Meredith, *Last Poems*; Pound, *Exultations and Personae*; death of Swinburne and Meredith
	1910 Awarded Order of Merit by King George V; Florence Dugdale lives at Max Gate as his secretary	**1910** Yeats, *Poems: Second Series*
	1912 Emma dies on 27 November; leads to the *Poems of 1912–13*	**1912** Pound, *Ripostes*
	1913 Revisits Cornwall and Plymouth	**1913** D. H. Lawrence, *Sons and Lovers*
1914 Outbreak of First World War	**1914** Marries Florence; publishes *Satires of Circumstance, Lyrics and Reveries*	
	1915 Death of Thomas Hardy's sister Mary	
	1916 Publication of *Selected Poems*	

World events

1918 First World War ends, with over 8 million dead worldwide

1923 Civil war in Russia ends with the Union of Soviet Socialist Republics

1925 Creation of the British Broadcasting Corporation

1926 The General Strike in Britain

Author's life

1918 Publishes *Moments of Vision and Miscellaneous Verses*; begins work on autobiography, *The Life of Thomas Hardy*, with Florence

1919 Publication of *Collected Poems*

1920 Receives honorary degree from Oxford University

1922 Publishes *Late Lyrics and Earlier*

1923 Prince of Wales visits Max Gate

1925 Publication of *Human Shows, Far Phantasies, Songs and Trifles*

1928 Dies on 11 January; heart buried in Stinsford Churchyard, ashes in Westminster Abbey

1937 Death of Florence Hardy

Literary events

1917 Robert Graves, *Fairies and Fusiliers*; death of Edward Thomas

1918 Thomas, *Last Poems*

1919 Siegfried Sassoon, *The War Poems*

1920 T. S. Eliot, *Poems*; Graves, *Country Sentiment*

1922 Eliot, *The Waste Land*; Blunden, *The Shepherd and Other Poems*; Yeats, *Later Poems*; birth of Philip Larkin

1923 Blunden, *To Nature*

1925 Virginia Woolf, *Mrs Dalloway*

1928 Yeats, *The Tower*; Blunden, *Japanese Garland*, *Retreat* and *Winter Nights*

WORKS OF THOMAS HARDY

NOVELS BY THOMAS HARDY

Desperate Remedies (1871)

Under the Greenwood Tree (1872)

A Pair of Blue Eyes (1873)

Far from the Madding Crowd (1874)

The Hand of Ethelberta (1876)

The Return of the Native (1878)

The Trumpet Major (1880)

A Laodicean (1881)

Two on a Tower (1882)

The Mayor of Casterbridge (1886)

The Woodlanders (1887)

Tess of the d'Urbervilles (1891)

The Well-Beloved (1892)

Jude the Obscure (1895)

SHORT-STORY COLLECTIONS BY THOMAS HARDY

Wessex Tales (1888)

A Group of Noble Dames (1891)

Life's Little Ironies (1894)

A Changed Man, The Waiting Supper, and Other Tales (largely reprints of earlier short works, 1913)

DRAMA BY THOMAS HARDY

The Dynasts; an epic-drama of the war with Napoleon (1904, 1906 and 1908)

The Famous Tragedy of the Queen of Cornwall (1923)

LITERARY CRITICISM

Joseph Bristow, *The Cambridge Companion to Victorian Poetry*, Cambridge Companions to Literature, Cambridge University Press, 2000
> Critical introduction to major figures and hitherto neglected women poets

Daniel Brown, *English Prose of the Nineteenth Century*, Longman Literature in English Series, Longman, 1997
> Wide-ranging survey covering nineteenth-century prose from various fields

R. G. Cox, ed., *Thomas Hardy: The Critical Heritage*, Routledge & Kegan Paul, 1970
> Includes early reviews of Hardy's poetry

Richard Cronin, Anthony Harrison and Alison Chapman, *A Companion to Victorian Poetry*, Blackwell Companions to Literature and Culture, Blackwell, 2002
> Scholarly essays which bring modern theoretical approaches to bear on the diversity of Victorian poetry

Donald Davie, *Thomas Hardy and British Poetry*, Oxford University Press, 1972
> Illuminating discussion of Hardy's poetry by a poet and academic

——, *Modernist Essays: Yeats, Pound and Eliot*, Carcanet Press Ltd, 2004
> Includes sensitive analyses of individual poems

Alex Davis and Lee M. Jenkins, *The Cambridge Companion to Modernist Poetry*, Cambridge Companions to Literature, Cambridge University Press, 2007
> An excellent introduction offering an overview and consideration of individual poets

Ralph Elliott, *Thomas Hardy's English*, Blackwell, 1984
> The most comprehensive guide to Hardy's language

James Gibson and Trevor Johnson, eds, *Thomas Hardy: Poems*, Macmillan Casebook (1979), 1991
> Essays on various aspects of Hardy's poetry

Timothy Hands, *Thomas Hardy*, Macmillan, 1995
> Valuable because it discusses writers who influenced Hardy's poetry

Geoffrey Harvey, *The Complete Critical Guide to Thomas Hardy*, Routledge, 2003
> Basic information about Hardy's life, contexts and works including a survey of critical interpretations

Trevor Johnson, *A Critical Introduction to the Poems of Thomas Hardy*, Macmillan, 1991
> Astute and accessible discussion of Hardy's poetry

Dale Kramer, ed., *The Cambridge Companion to Thomas Hardy*, Cambridge University Press, 1999
> Includes 'Wessex' by Simon Gatrell as well as the complementary essays 'Hardy as a Nineteenth-century Poet' by Dennis Taylor and 'The Modernity of Thomas Hardy's Poetry' by John Paul Riquelme

Philip Larkin, *Required Writing: Miscellaneous Pieces 1955–1982*, Faber, 1983
> Includes the essay 'Wanted: Good Hardy Critic' which originally appeared in *Critical Quarterly*, vol. 8, no. 2, summer 1966

F. R. Leavis, *New Bearings in English Poetry*, Chatto & Windus, 1932
> Alternately perceptive and limited discussion of Hardy's poetry which adversely influenced a generation of critical estimations

John Lucas, *Modern English Poetry from Hardy to Hughes*, Batsford, 1986
> From an explicitly socialist critical perspective, Hardy is celebrated as a poet of community and human solidarity

J. Hillis Miller and Julian Wolfreys, *The J. Hillis Miller Reader*, Stanford University Press, 2005
> The essay entitled 'Hardy' offers a deconstructive reading of Hardy's poetry

Francis O'Gorman, *A Concise Companion to the Victorian Novel*, Concise Companions to Literature and Culture, Blackwell, 2004
> Essays by Victorian scholars which locate texts in Victorian cultural contexts

Tom Paulin, *Thomas Hardy: The Poetry of Perception*, Macmillan, 1975
> Hardy's poetic career and craft including detailed readings of the poems

F. B. Pinion, *A Commentary on the Poems of Thomas Hardy*, Macmillan, 1976
> Poem-by-poem commentary including useful background information

Bernard Richards, *English Poetry of the Victorian Period 1830–1890*, Longman Literature in English Series, Longman, 1988
> Thematically structured with detailed analysis of individual poets

C. K. Stead, *Pound, Yeats, Eliot and the Modernist Movement*, Palgrave Macmillan, 1986
> Useful introduction to modernist poetry

Dennis Taylor, *Hardy's Poetry 1860–1928*, Clarendon Press, 1981
> Astute and illuminating account of Hardy's career and poetic craft

——, *Hardy's Metres and Victorian Prosody*, Macmillan, 1988
> The authoritative work on Hardy's metrics

Further reading

J. P. Ward, *Thomas Hardy's Poetry*, Open University Press, 1992
> Examines Hardy's place in a poetic tradition which includes Wordsworth, John Clare, Robert Frost and Philip Larkin

Michael Wheeler, *English Fiction of the Victorian Period 1830–1890*, Longman Literature in English Series, Longman, 1985
> Covers major and minor novelists in the context of the age

Peter Widdowson, *On Thomas Hardy: Late Essays and Earlier*, Macmillan, 1998
> Includes the essay 'Re-casting Hardy the Poet' (1996)

Paul Zeitlow, *Moments of Vision: The Poetry of Thomas Hardy*, Harvard University Press, 1974
> Systematic study of a large number of poems

Biography and autobiography

Robert Gittings, *Young Thomas Hardy* (1975), and *The Older Hardy* (1978), Heinemann Educational
> Controversial because often unsympathetic but very readable

Emma Hardy, *Some Recollections*, ed. Evelyn Hardy and Robert Gittings, Oxford University Press, 1979
> Emma's memoir which Hardy drew on for several poems

Florence Emily Hardy, *The Life of Thomas Hardy, 1840-1928*, Macmillan, 1975
> The one-volume edition of *The Early Life of Thomas Hardy, 1840-1891* (1928) and *The Later Years of Thomas Hardy, 1892–1928* (1930)

Michael Millgate, *Thomas Hardy: A Biography*, Oxford University Press, 1982
> Considered to be the definitive biography

——, *The Life and Work of Thomas Hardy by F. E. Hardy*, Macmillan, 1985
> Claims to be the original text of Hardy's autobiography (*The Early Life* and *The Later Years*) before Florence Hardy altered it for publication

Claire Tomalin, *Thomas Hardy*, Penguin Press, 2007
> Has the virtue of concentrating on the poetry, and offers some useful insights

Paul Turner, *The Life of Thomas Hardy: A Critical Biography*, Blackwell, 1998
> Valuable because it examines Hardy's reading and its influence on his work

WIDER READING

For connections and comparisons with the poetry of Thomas Hardy see the relevant pages of these Notes (provided in bold below).

VICTORIAN POETRY

Alfred, Lord Tennyson, *Idylls of the King*, 1842–85 **(p. 26)**; *In Memoriam*, 1833–50 **(pp. 31, 93, 104)**

Matthew Arnold, *New Poems*, 1867 **(p. 17)**

William Barnes, *Select Poems*, 1908 **(p. 49)**; see also *Poems of Rural Life in the Dorset Dialect*, 1844

Robert Browning, *Men and Women*, 1855 **(pp. 38, 99)**

Algernon Charles Swinburne, *Atalanta in Calydon*, 1865 **(p. 128)**; *Poems and Ballads*, 1866 **(p. 128)**; 'The Transvaal', 1899 **(p. 14)**

MODERNIST POETRY

T. S. Eliot, *Poems*, 1920; *The Waste Land*, 1922 **(pp. 110, 128)**

Ezra Pound, *Cantos*, 1925–69 **(p. 110)**

W. B. Yeats, *Collected Works*, 1908 **(p. 110)**

VICTORIAN PROSE (FICTION AND NON-FICTION)

Arnold Bennett, *Anna of the Five Towns*, 1902 **(p. 125)**

Charlotte Brontë, *Jane Eyre* 1847 **(p. 115)**

Emily Brontë, *Wuthering Heights*, 1847 **(p. 115)**

Charles Darwin, *On the Origin of Species by Means of Natural Selection: or, The Preservation of Favoured Races in the Struggle for Life*, 1859 **(pp. 75, 87, 116)**

Charles Dickens, *Bleak House*, 1853 **(p. 84)**

——, *Great Expectations*, 1861 **(pp. 18, 84)**

George Eliot, *Adam Bede*, 1859 **(p. 125)**

Gustave Flaubert, *Madame Bovary*, 1857 **(p. 126)**

Elizabeth Gaskell, *Mary Barton*, 1848 **(p. 18)**

Further Reading

George Gissing, *New Grub Street*, 1891 **(p. 125)**

J. S. Mill, *On Liberty*, 1859 **(pp. 77, 116)**

George Moore, *A Modern Lover*, 1883 **(p. 125)**

John Ruskin, *The Stones of Venice*, 1853 **(p. 91)**

Robert Louis Stevenson, *The Strange Case of Dr Jekyll and Mr Hyde*, 1886 **(p. 125)**

Leo Tolstoy, *Anna Karenina*, 1873–7 **(p. 126)**

Emile Zola, *Germinal*, 1885 **(p. 126)**

Drama
Henrik Ibsen, *A Doll's House*, 1879 **(p. 83)**

W. B. Yeats, *The Countess Cathleen*, 1892 **(p. 110)**

LITERARY TERMS

alienation the sense of being separated from, or adrift within, one's environment or social context

alliteration a sequence of repeated consonantal sounds in a stretch of language, e.g. the repeated 'r' sound in 'And the rotten rose is ript from the wall' ('During Wind and Rain'). The matching consonants are usually at the beginning of words or stressed syllables

allusion a passing reference in a work of literature to something outside itself (such as another work of literature, a legend, a cultural belief or a historical fact)

anachronism a person, custom or event which does not belong in the historical period in which it is placed; something which is out of harmony with its period

anapaest in English **versification** an anapaest is a trisyllabic metrical **foot** consisting of two unstressed syllables followed by a stressed syllable (ti-ti-tum). For example, 'When the Present has latched its postern behind my tremulous stay' is a **hexameter** with a combination of **iambic** and anapaestic feet

anthology a collection of works (usually poetry) by different authors

antithetical a style which deliberately patterns material in an oppositional way so as to highlight contrasts

assonance the correspondence, or near-correspondence, in two words of the **stressed** vowel, and sometimes those which follow (but – unlike **rhyme** – not of the consonants). For example, 'The home-bound foot-folk wrap their snow-flaked heads' in 'The Five Students'. Assonance can be described as the vowel equivalent of **alliteration**

ballad a traditional poem or song which tells a story in simple, **colloquial** language. A ballad's story, which is often **tragic** in nature (as in 'A Trampwoman's Tragedy'), is told through dialogue and action, while structural features typically include **refrains** and **incremental repetition**

ballad metre a **quatrain** of alternate four-**stress** and three-stress lines, usually roughly **iambic**, rhymed either abcb or abab (also known as **common measure**)

bathos a ludicrous descent from the elevated treatment of a subject to the ordinary and commonplace

cadences the rising and falling rhythms of speech which writers of poetry and prose often reproduce

caesura (pl. **caesurae**) a pause within a line of poetry, caused by the natural organisation of the language into phrases, clauses and sentences, which do not conform to the natural metrical pattern

canon a literary canon is a body of writings by approved by critics as worthy of study

cliché a widely used expression which, through over-use, has lost impact and originality

colloquialism the use of the kinds of expression and grammar associated with ordinary, everyday speech rather than formal language

common measure another term for **ballad metre**

compound epithet hyphenated adjectival phrase used to describe the unique aspects of a person, animal or thing; sometimes known as the Homeric epithet after its use by the author of the early Greek epics *The Odyssey* and *The Illiad* in examples such as 'the wine-dark sea' and 'rosy-fingered Dawn'

couplet a pair of consecutive lines of poetry which **rhyme** together

cycle a group of poems, plays, stories or novels which are grouped together, either by the author or by tradition, and which all deal, more or less, with some central theme or themes. See also **elegy**

dactyl in English **versification**, a type of metrical **foot** which consists of a strongly stressed syllable followed by two weak ones (tum-ti-ti), as in 'The Voice', where the line 'Woman much missed, how you call to me, call to me' is a dactylic **tetrameter**

dialect the particular style and manner of speaking of a specified area, nation or social class

diction the choice of words in a work of literature: the kind of vocabulary used

dimeter a line of poetry consisting of two metrical **feet** (i.e. two main **stresses**), for example the line 'And feeling fled' from 'At Castle Boterel'. Dimeters are rarely used except in conjunction with other line-lengths

dramatic monologue a specific kind of poem in which a single person, not the poet, is the 'speaker'

eclecticism in the arts, especially music and architecture (and notably in literature in the late twentieth century), the practice of drawing on ideas, methods and styles from various sources when creating a new work, often without much regard for consistency and harmony

egotistical sublime a phrase used by John Keats (1795–1821) to describe what he considered to be the excessively self-centred quality of William Wordsworth's poetry

elegy a poem of lamentation, usually focusing on the death of a single person. More generally, the term 'elegy' can also be used to describe any gravely meditative work of poetry.

Many elegies follow a conventional pattern, or cycle of sections meant to emulate the phases of mourning, which initially register shock at the death, followed by despair, resignation and, finally, reconciliation

epic a long narrative poem in an elevated style; typical epic themes include myth, legend, and the birth and destruction of nations

epigraph a quotation or fragment placed by a writer at the beginning of a poem, novel or chapter as a clue or hint towards its meaning

epitaph an inscription on a tomb, or a piece of writing suitable for that purpose

existential the adjective derived from the noun 'existentialism', a philosophy expressed in much twentieth-century literature, which argues that, in the absence of God, the only meaning in life is that which individual humans create for themselves

feminine ending a line of poetry which ends on an unstressed syllable (see **metre**)

feminine rhyme rhymed words of two or more syllables, where the last syllable is not **stressed**, also known as double rhyme

foot in order to determine the metre of a line of poetry, it is necessary to divide it into feet, which are certain fixed combinations of weakly and strongly stressed syllables, such as **anapaests, dactyls, iambs** and **trochees**

free verse unrhymed verse without a standard **metre**. Although it can be very rhythmical, a poem in free verse cannot be resolved into the regular lines of repeated **feet** which characterise traditional **versification**. It was developed extensively in the twentieth century, particularly by **modernists** such as T. S. Eliot and Ezra Pound

heptameter a line of poetry consisting of seven metrical **feet**, i.e. seven main **stresses**

heroic couplet pair of rhyming lines of **iambic** pentameter

hexameter a line of poetry consisting of six metrical **feet**, i.e. six main **stresses**, as in 'The Immanent Will that stirs and urges everything' from 'The Convergence of the Twain'

iamb the commonest metrical **foot** in English **versification**, consisting of a weak stress followed by a strong stress (ti-tum). 'So fair a fancy few would weave' (from 'The Oxen') is an example of an iambic **tetrameter**

ideology the collection of ideas, opinions, values, beliefs and preconceptions which combine to make up the 'mind-set' of a group of people, that is, the intellectual framework through which they view everything, and which colours all their attitudes and feelings. The term is particularly used to refer to people's assumptions about power and authority

imagery in its narrowest sense an image is a picture in words – a description of some visible scene or object. More commonly, however, 'imagery' refers to the figurative language in a work of literature, such as **metaphors** and **similes**; or all the words which refer to objects and qualities which appeal to the senses and feelings

imagism a self-conscious literary movement in Britain and the United States initiated by Ezra Pound and T. E. Hulme in 1912. The imagists valued directness of language in short **lyric** poems, usually constructed around single **images,** and exploiting **juxtaposition**

impersonality the quality in literature of having no sense of the writer's personality and no personal tone or references

incremental repetition a term used to describe the use of a repeated **refrain** in poems, especially **ballads,** which is altered from one **stanza** to the next so as to fit in with the story or comment on the action. In 'The Five Students', for example, the fifth line of each stanza is a refrain, which is modified each time one of the characters is lost

irony a use of language, widespread in all kinds of literature and everyday speech, which is characterised by saying or writing one thing while another is meant

juxtapose to place items side by side sometimes jarringly in order to make a point by sharp contrast

lament a poem expressing deep sorrow for the death of a person or people, or loss of status and security

lyric a poem, usually short, expressing in a personal manner the feelings and thoughts of an individual speaker

masculine ending a line of poetry which ends on a **stressed** syllable. For example, 'At Castle Boterel' has alternating masculine and **feminine endings**

masculine rhyme a monosyllabic rhyme on the final stressed syllables of two lines of poetry

memoir an autobiography or a written account of one's memories, focusing on events witnessed and people known rather than on aspects of one's life and individuality

metaphor derived from the Greek meaning 'carrying over', a figure of speech in which a word or phrase is applied to an object, a character or an action which does not literally belong to it, in order to imply a resemblance and create an unusual or striking image in the reader's mind

metre the pattern of **stresses** occurring (more or less regularly) in lines of poetry and arranged within a fixed total number of syllables (although a **feminine ending** is an accepted variation). Combinations of stressed and unstressed syllables are referred to as **feet**

modernism a term applied to experimental trends in literature (and other arts) in the early twentieth century; in poetry the reader is often challenged to deduce meaning from a collage of fragmentary **images** and complex **allusions**

motif a literary device, such as a theme, **image** or **symbol**, which recurs frequently, either within a body of literature or within a single work

Movement, the name for a group of poets of the 1950s whose work was collected in the **anthology** *New Lines* (1956) by Robert Conquest. Contributors included Philip Larkin, Thom Gunn, Ted Hughes and Elizabeth Jennings; they found common ground in a move away from the perceived excesses of **modernism** towards the poetic qualities of intelligence, control and verbal dexterity, combined with wit, clarity and a certain modesty of ambition

narrative a story, tale or any recital of events, and the manner in which it is told

narrator the character (as distinct from the poet) in a **ballad** or other narrative poem who tells the story

neologism the coining of a new word; an innovation in language

objective correlative a term used by T. S. Eliot to describe an external equivalent for an internal state of mind. An objective correlative is thus any object, scene, event or situation that may be said to stand for or evoke a given mood or emotion, as opposed to a direct subjective expression of it

oeuvre the French word for 'work' and used to describe the collected writings of an author considered as a whole

onomatopeia the use of words whose sounds echo the noises they describe

paradox a seemingly absurd or self-contradictory statement that is or may be true

pastiche imitation of the style of writing of an earlier author

pastoral an escapist mode of writing which describes the innocence of shepherds and shepherdesses in contrast to the corruptions of city life

patriarchy a system of society or government ruled by men and usually organised for the convenience of men

pentameter a line of poetry consisting of five metrical **feet**, i. e. five main **stresses**. When these feet are basically **iambic** the result is the commonest line form in English poetry, as in 'This candle-wax is shaping to a shroud' from 'Standing by the Mantlepiece'

persona (pl. **personae**) an identity assumed by a writer in a literary work (in Latin, a 'mask'): a means of writing from a perspective not one's own. See also **impersonality**

personification a variety of figurative or **metaphorical** language in which things or ideas are treated as if they were human beings, with human attributes and feelings. In 'The Five Students', for example, Hardy writes that 'The sun grows passionate-eyed'

Petrarchan sonnet a form of **sonnet** made up of an octave (a group of eight lines) and a sestet (a group of six lines) with the **rhyme scheme** abbaabba cdecde (or sometimes abbaabba cdcdcd)

prosody the science of **versification**: the study of the theory and development of **metres** and **stanza** forms

quatrain a **stanza** of four lines

refrain words or lines recurring at intervals in the course of a poem, sometimes with slight variation, usually at the end of a **stanza**; they are especially common in songs and **ballads**

rhetoric originally the art of speaking (and writing) effectively so as to persuade an audience; the term is now often used to cover the whole range of literary and linguistic devices. The term 'rhetorical question' is used to refer to a question asked not for the sake of enquiry but for emphasis, when the writer or speaker expects the reader or audience to be totally convinced about the appropriate reply

rhyme though by no means all verse is rhymed, rhyme is one of the most striking and obvious differences between verse and prose, and the most easily identified common aspect of English **versification**. It consists of chiming or matching sounds at the ends of lines of poetry, which create a very clearly audible sense of pattern

rhyme scheme the pattern of **rhymes** within a **stanza** or section of a poem, usually expressed by an alphabetical code (e.g. 'aabb') in which identical letters indicate the lines which rhyme

rhythm in English poetry and prose the chief element of rhythm is the variation in levels of **stress** accorded to the syllables in a particular stretch of language; in poetry the rhythm is more or less controlled and regular (see **metre**)

Romantic the 'r' is usually capitalised (as here) to distinguish the popular usage of the word 'romantic' from a convenient term of English literary history used to denote the period from 1789 (the French Revolution) to about 1830. Principal English Romantic writers included Wordsworth, Coleridge, Byron, Keats and Shelley

rondeau an elaborate **verse form,** French in origin and usually playful in subject matter. A rondeau typically consists of thirteen lines, employing only two **rhymes,** plus a **refrain:** the first word or opening phrase is repeated after the eighth and the thirteenth lines

sardonic usually, an ironic tone of voice which sees the grim humour in potentially tragic situations; occasionally denoting mocking or sarcastic laughter at someone's supposed failings

satire a type of literature in which folly, evil or topical issues are held up to scorn through ridicule, **irony** or exaggeration

simile a species of figurative writing involving a direct comparison of one thing to another. Similes typically make use of the words 'like' or 'as', for example 'The tangled bine-stems scored the sky, / Like strings of broken lyres' in 'The Darkling Thrush'

sonnet a **lyric** poem of fixed form: fourteen lines of **iambic pentameter** which are **rhymed** and organised according to one of several intricate schemes. They often comprise an octave (eight lines) and a sestet (six lines), or three **quatrains** and a **couplet**

stanza a unit of several lines of poetry; a repeated group of lines of poetry. What distinguishes a stanza from simply any section of poetry is the fact that it is a regular and repeated aspect of the poem's shape

stereotype a standard, fixed idea or mental impression; a **cliché** or stock character

stress in any word of more than one syllable, more emphasis or loudness will be given to one of the syllables in comparison with the others; in English poetry, the **metre** of a line is determined by regular patterns of stressed syllables in a sequence of stressed and unstressed syllables

symbol something which represents something else by analogy or association. For example, Hardy often viewed the railway as a symbol of nineteenth-century 'progress': it is used in this way in 'Places', where the 'urgent clack' of the present day suggests the noise of a train passing along the track

syntax the grammatical structure of sentences

tetrameter a line of poetry consisting of four metrical **feet,** i.e. four main **stresses,** as in 'We stood by a pond that winter day' from 'Neutral Tones'

tragedy although technically 'tragedy' refers to a genre of drama, in general literary usage the term can refer to any work which traces the downfall of an individual, particularly if this downfall illustrates both the capacities and the limitations of human life

trimeter a line of poetry consisting of three metrical **feet,** i.e. three main **stresses,** as in 'In a solitude of the sea' from 'The Convergence of the Twain'

triple rhyme a **rhyme** on three syllables, for example 'listlessness' and 'wistlessness' in 'The Voice'

trochee in English **versification** a trochee is a **foot** consisting of a strongly **stressed** syllable followed by a weakly stressed syllable

verse form a repeated pattern in terms of line length, **metre** and **rhyme** of **stanzas** which compose a poem. This includes fixed poetic forms such as the **sonnet,** the **rondeau,** etc.

versification the study of the art of writing **metrically** (and with attention not only to **metre,** but **rhythm, rhyme** and **stanza** form); also, the act of composition of poetry

Victorian a term referring to the reign of Queen Victoria (1837–1901). It is often regarded as a homogeneous literary period, but in reality it manifested huge changes in society, outlook and literary output

vignettes essays or short stories which have a single point to make; sometimes brief prose descriptions which seek to capture the essence of a person or place

Alan Pound is a former Head of English at St Martin's College, Lancaster (now the University of Cumbria). Since 2003 he has taught in the English Department at the University of Wisconsin-River Falls, USA. His research interests lie primarily in the field of Victorian literature, and he has also co-authored an edition of William Blake's poetry.

NOTES

NOTES

GCSE

Maya Angelou
I Know Why the Caged Bird Sings

Jane Austen
Pride and Prejudice

Alan Ayckbourn
Absent Friends

Elizabeth Barrett Browning
Selected Poems

Robert Bolt
A Man for All Seasons

Harold Brighouse
Hobson's Choice

Charlotte Brontë
Jane Eyre

Emily Brontë
Wuthering Heights

Brian Clark
Whose Life is it Anyway?

Robert Cormier
Heroes

Shelagh Delaney
A Taste of Honey

Charles Dickens
David Copperfield
Great Expectations
Hard Times
Oliver Twist
Selected Stories

Roddy Doyle
Paddy Clarke Ha Ha Ha

George Eliot
Silas Marner
The Mill on the Floss

Anne Frank
The Diary of a Young Girl

William Golding
Lord of the Flies

Oliver Goldsmith
She Stoops to Conquer

Willis Hall
The Long and the Short and the Tall

Thomas Hardy
Far from the Madding Crowd
The Mayor of Casterbridge
Tess of the d'Urbervilles
The Withered Arm and other Wessex Tales

L. P. Hartley
The Go-Between

Seamus Heaney
Selected Poems

Susan Hill
I'm the King of the Castle

Barry Hines
A Kestrel for a Knave

Louise Lawrence
Children of the Dust

Harper Lee
To Kill a Mockingbird

Laurie Lee
Cider with Rosie

Arthur Miller
The Crucible
A View from the Bridge

Robert O'Brien
Z for Zachariah

Frank O'Connor
My Oedipus Complex and Other Stories

George Orwell
Animal Farm

J. B. Priestley
An Inspector Calls
When We Are Married

Willy Russell
Educating Rita
Our Day Out

J. D. Salinger
The Catcher in the Rye

William Shakespeare
Henry IV Part I
Henry V
Julius Caesar
Macbeth
The Merchant of Venice
A Midsummer Night's Dream
Much Ado About Nothing
Romeo and Juliet
The Tempest
Twelfth Night

George Bernard Shaw
Pygmalion

Mary Shelley
Frankenstein

R. C. Sherriff
Journey's End

Rukshana Smith
Salt on the Snow

John Steinbeck
Of Mice and Men

Robert Louis Stevenson
Dr Jekyll and Mr Hyde

Jonathan Swift
Gulliver's Travels

Robert Swindells
Daz 4 Zoe

Mildred D. Taylor
Roll of Thunder, Hear My Cry

Mark Twain
Huckleberry Finn

James Watson
Talking in Whispers

Edith Wharton
Ethan Frome

William Wordsworth
Selected Poems
A Choice of Poets
Mystery Stories of the Nineteenth Century including The Signalman
Nineteenth Century Short Stories
Poetry of the First World War
Six Women Poets
For the AQA Anthology:
Duffy and Armitage & Pre-1914 Poetry
Heaney and Clarke & Pre-1914 Poetry
Poems from Different Cultures

Key Stage 3

William Shakespeare
Henry V
Macbeth
Much Ado About Nothing
Richard III
The Tempest

Margaret Atwood
Cat's Eye
The Handmaid's Tale
Jane Austen
Emma
Mansfield Park
Persuasion
Pride and Prejudice
Sense and Sensibility
William Blake
Songs of Innocence and of Experience
The Brontës
Selected Poems
Charlotte Brontë
Jane Eyre
Villette
Emily Brontë
Wuthering Heights
Angela Carter
The Bloody Chamber
Nights at the Circus
Wise Children
Geoffrey Chaucer
The Franklin's Prologue and Tale
The Merchant's Prologue and Tale
The Miller's Prologue and Tale
The Pardoner's Tale
The Prologue to the Canterbury Tales
The Wife of Bath's Prologue and Tale
Caryl Churchill
Top Girls
John Clare
Selected Poems
Joseph Conrad
Heart of Darkness
Charles Dickens
Bleak House
Great Expectations
Hard Times
Emily Dickinson
Selected Poems
Carol Ann Duffy
Selected Poems
The World's Wife
George Eliot
Middlemarch
The Mill on the Floss
T. S. Eliot
Selected Poems
The Waste Land

F. Scott Fitzgerald
The Great Gatsby
John Ford
'Tis Pity She's a Whore
E. M. Forster
A Passage to India
Michael Frayn
Spies
Charles Frazier
Cold Mountain
Brian Friel
Making History
Translations
William Golding
The Spire
Thomas Hardy
Jude the Obscure
The Mayor of Casterbridge
The Return of the Native
Selected Poems
Tess of the d'Urbervilles
Nathaniel Hawthorne
The Scarlet Letter
Seamus Heaney
Selected Poems from 'Opened Ground'
Homer
The Iliad
The Odyssey
Aldous Huxley
Brave New World
Henrik Ibsen
A Doll's House
Kazuo Ishiguro
The Remains of the Day
James Joyce
Dubliners
John Keats
Selected Poems
Philip Larkin
High Windows
The Whitsun Weddings and Selected Poems
Ian McEwan
Atonement
Christopher Marlowe
Doctor Faustus
Edward II
Arthur Miller
All My Sons
Death of a Salesman
John Milton
Paradise Lost Books I & II

Toni Morrison
Beloved
George Orwell
Nineteen Eighty-Four
Sylvia Plath
Selected Poems
William Shakespeare
Antony and Cleopatra
As You Like It
Hamlet
Henry IV Part I
King Lear
Macbeth
Measure for Measure
The Merchant of Venice
A Midsummer Night's Dream
Much Ado About Nothing
Othello
Richard II
Richard III
Romeo and Juliet
The Taming of the Shrew
The Tempest
Twelfth Night
The Winter's Tale
Mary Shelley
Frankenstein
Richard Brinsley Sheridan
The School for Scandal
Bram Stoker
Dracula
Alfred Tennyson
Selected Poems
Alice Walker
The Color Purple
John Webster
The Duchess of Malfi
The White Devil
Oscar Wilde
The Importance of Being Earnest
A Woman of No Importance
Tennessee Williams
Cat on a Hot Tin Roof
The Glass Menagerie
A Streetcar Named Desire
Jeanette Winterson
Oranges Are Not the Only Fruit
Virginia Woolf
To the Lighthouse
William Wordsworth
The Prelude and Selected Poems
W. B. Yeats
Selected Poems
Poetry of the First World War